# Engaging Young Children With Informational Books

# Classroom Insights from Educational Psychology Series

# Engaging Young Children With Informational Books

Helen Patrick | Panayota Mantzicopoulos

A Joint Publication

## CORWIN
A SAGE Company

FOR INFORMATION:

Corwin

A SAGE Company

2455 Teller Road

Thousand Oaks, California 91320

(800) 233-9936

www.corwin.com

SAGE Publications Ltd.

1 Oliver's Yard

55 City Road

London EC1Y 1SP

United Kingdom

SAGE Publications India Pvt. Ltd.

B 1/I 1 Mohan Cooperative Industrial Area

Mathura Road, New Delhi 110 044

India

SAGE Publications Asia-Pacific Pte. Ltd.

3 Church Street

#10-04 Samsung Hub

Singapore 049483

Copyright © 2014 by Division 15 (Educational Psychology) of the APA

Printed in the United States of America.

*A catalog record of this book is available from the Library of Congress.*

ISBN: 978-1-4129-8670-0

A Joint Publication With APA Division 15: Educational Psychology

This book is printed on acid-free paper.

Acquisitions Editor: Jessica Allan

Associate Editor: Kimberly Greenberg

Editorial Assistant: Heidi Arndt

Project Editor: Veronica Stapleton Hooper

Copy Editor: Amy Rosenstein

Typesetter: C&M Digitals (P) Ltd.

Proofreader: Sarah J. Duffy

Indexer: Sheila Bodell

Cover Designer: Karine Hovsepian

MIX
Paper from responsible sources
FSC
www.fsc.org
FSC® C014174

13 14 15 16 17 10 9 8 7 6 5 4 3 2 1

# Contents

# Series Preface to Classroom Insights

**D**ivision 15, Educational Psychology, of the American Psychological Association and Corwin partnered to create the Classroom Insights from Educational Psychology series for teachers in an effort to reduce the widening gap between research and theory on learning, teaching, and classroom practice. Educational psychology is a discipline that seeks to understand the integration among human development and learning, classroom learning environments and instructional strategies, and student learning and assessment. In this way, the field of educational psychology is among the most relevant and applicable for teachers.

Although we have seen great advances in our understanding of student learning and instructional practices over the last decade, these advances are not highly visible in today's classrooms, preservice and graduate teacher education programs, or professional development for teachers. Consequently, classroom practice for the most part does not seem to be highly influenced by current research and theory in educational psychology. Yet there are international calls for "scientifically based practices," "research-based methods," or "evidence-based decisions" in our schools. As part of the solution to this problem, this series of short, easily accessible books for teachers is designed to synthesize in-depth, high-quality research to be used in a variety of educational settings, and it is endorsed by Division 15.

As the Classroom Insights series evolves from its first volumes under founding editor Dr. Barbara McCombs, we as editors continue to work with teachers and researchers to identify the topics that are most relevant to educators. We are guided by research that honors the highest quality learning environments with practices proven to support all students, help them succeed in their schooling, and sustain their love of learning. The goals of this series are threefold:

- To give practicing and preservice teachers access to current advances in research and theory on classroom teaching and learning in an easily understood and usable form
- To align educator preparation, graduate study, and professional development with current advances in research and theory, which have not been widely shared with teachers
- To highlight how the most effective teaching practices are based upon a substantial research base and created within classrooms, rather than applied in a "one-size-fits-all" or "silver-bullet" approach across classrooms

Classroom Insights provides a series of specialized books to inform teaching and learning in PK–12 classrooms by focusing on what is most important and relevant to today's teachers. In some volumes, the applications are limited to specific age levels or characteristics of students, while in most volumes the ideas can be broadly applied across PK–12 settings. Classroom strategies are integrated throughout every book, and each one includes a wide array of resources for teachers to use to study their practices and improve student achievement and classroom learning environments. Finally, many of these research-based applications will be new approaches and frameworks that have never been published in a series for teachers.

As series editors, our goal is to provide the most up-to-date professional series of teacher resources for connecting teachers with the highest quality and most relevant research in our field of educational psychology. We have planned for every page to provide useful insights for teachers into their current practices to transform classroom learning for their students, themselves, and their school communities.

Debra K. Meyer, PhD
Professor
Elmhurst College

Lynley H. Anderman, PhD
Professor
The Ohio State University

# Acknowledgments

**W**e wish to thank the teachers, children, and parents who participated in our studies over the past several years. They taught us much about learning from informational texts.

Special thanks go to our editor, Deb Meyer. Her positivity, patience, and constructive comments were invaluable during the writing process.

Our deep appreciation goes to our families, who supported us throughout our research journeys.

We dedicate this book to our children: Simon, Ben, Dimitri, and Costa. Their questions about the world and their early interest in informational texts sparked our enthusiasm and involvement in this area of research.

## PUBLISHER'S ACKNOWLEDGMENTS

Corwin gratefully acknowledges the contributions of the following reviewers:

**Renee Boss**
NBCT and Secondary English Language Arts Specialist
Fayette County Public Schools
Lexington, KY

**Nina Orellana**
Title 1 Teacher
Palm Bay Academy Charter School
Palm Bay, FL

**Robert E. Yager**
Professor of Science Education
University of Iowa
Iowa City, IA

# About the Authors

**Dr. Helen Patrick** is a professor of educational psychology in Purdue University's College of Education. Her teaching and research focus on creating positive classroom environments that promote students' learning, understanding, and motivation. She has worked in numerous elementary schools in Michigan, Illinois, and Indiana. Most recently, she has worked with teachers and children in ethnically diverse kindergartens, focusing on ways to successfully integrate teaching "big ideas" of science with reading and writing activities. Read more about this Scientific Literacy Project, funded by the U.S. Department of Education, at http://www.purduescientificliteracyproject.org.

**Dr. Panayota (Youli) Mantzicopoulos** is professor of educational psychology in Purdue University's College of Education. Her interests include early personal-social development and learning in diverse environments. Her research has examined the effectiveness of early grade-retention practices, the development of self-competence beliefs, early teacher-child relationships, and shared reading of informational texts as a context for learning both at home and school. Her most recent work has been associated with the Scientific Literacy Project (http://www .purduescientificliteracyproject.org), where she has focused on the integration of informational texts with science inquiry activities and on investigating the development of children's socially derived meanings about science. Visit her at https://collaborate .education.purdue.edu/edst/youli/default.aspx.

# Introduction

The adage "learn to read and then read to learn" sums up what has long seemed a sensible approach to education. Reading is, after all, crucial for our everyday activities and is a part of all other academic subjects. Therefore, reading and the language arts have held a privileged position in the early school years, with fictional stories being predominant. Significant and meaningful instructional time for content areas such as social studies and science is typically allocated only once children have mastered reading, after third grade. It has become evident, however, that although focusing primarily on reading instruction during the first few years may sound a reasonable course of action, it actually sets children up for significant problems in the upper elementary grades and beyond. In particular, children's unfamiliarity with instructional text and with the content knowledge that is usually presented in informational books leads to too many children struggling to understand informational text and learn subjects such as science.

Children need to have early and positive learning and emotional experiences in the subjects and skill areas in which competence and motivation are important for school and beyond. Without experiencing nonfiction books, children will not be sufficiently familiar with the genre-specific skills needed to read and understand the informational texts that present social studies and science content. Children in the early grades need to read and learn about geography, history, technology, or science intentionally (i.e., more than as a result of sporadic out-of-school experiences) so they develop background knowledge and vocabulary in these subjects. Deficiencies in foundational knowledge and skills undermine children's interest and enjoyment in subject areas as well as their confidence that they can be successful in learning them. Therefore, without considerable experience with informational books, children will likely *not*

- develop the ability to comprehend informational text,
- be able to analyze and synthesize information and create reasoned and coherent arguments,
- have a sturdy base in the sciences and social studies that will support building the understanding necessary for people to be informed and literate citizens, and
- pursue subjects like science when they make educational and occupational choices, because those subjects are considered to be too difficult or not interesting.

Different professional organizations, representing a variety of interests, have expressed concerns that converge with the points we have just noted. We elaborate on these concerns next.

## CURRENT CONCERNS

### Insufficient skills to comprehend informational texts

The independent, not-for-profit organization ACT (2006) reported that only about half of American 12th graders have the reading skills needed "to enroll and succeed without remediation in credit-bearing entry level coursework at a two- or four-year college, trade school, or technical school" (p. 3). Insufficient skills for reading and understanding informational text are particularly problematic, because this genre represents the majority of reading required for higher education and work-related training programs (National Governors Association [NGA] Center for Best Practices & Council of Chief State School Officers [CCSSO], 2010). Business groups note that insufficient literacy skills are a major contributor to the current serious shortage of skilled workers (Institute for a Competitive Workforce, 2012), and the importance of being able to read, comprehend, and write informational text is not going to wane any time soon. The fastest growing professions require literacy skills that are higher than average, particularly in terms of informational texts (Sparks, 2012).

## Deficiencies in analysis, synthesis, and argumentation skills

Being able to analyze and synthesize information, think critically, solve problems in innovative ways, and learn new things are some of employers' most important considerations when hiring, rated even above subject-matter expertise (Institute for a Competitive Workforce, 2011). This reflects the reality that in order to keep up with the inevitable technological advances of the near future, workers will need more than just today's knowledge; they will need 21st century skills (National Research Council, 2010). These skills involve being able to think flexibly, develop and learn new information, seek out and make sense of a range of information, consider various perspectives, weigh different options, draw conclusions, and communicate them effectively to others. Inquiry activities, which involve students questioning, evaluating, organizing, analyzing, challenging, and synthesizing informational sources, are an especially effective context within which to develop these skills (National Research Council, 2012). Through engaging in inquiry, students can experience topics in social studies or science "as a weave of questions and interpretations" rather than "a staggering assemblage of facts" (Gewertz, 2012, p. 9).

## Too few skilled workers for an increasingly complex, technological, and global society

Many organizations warn that the United States is facing a shortage of workers in the STEM (science, technology, engineering, and mathematics) fields (National Academy of

Sciences, National Academy of Engineering, & Institute of Medicine, 2010). Furthermore, the current gap between supply and demand for skilled workers is expected to increase (U.S. Congress Joint Economic Committee, 2012). What is mentioned less often, however, is that because technology has permeated so many industries and occupations, even jobs that do not fall within a STEM field nevertheless require workers to be STEM-capable (U.S. Congress Joint Economic Committee, 2012). Therefore, it is important that all students graduate from high school with STEM skills and knowledge.

## COMMON CORE STATE STANDARDS

The newly developed Common Core State Standards (CCSS) for English language arts and literacy in history/social studies, science, and technical subjects (NGA & CCSSO, 2010) represent a comprehensive and cohesive response to addressing the concerns just outlined. A cornerstone of the standards is that students must develop literacy skills in multiple disciplines, from the beginning of school onward, so that "fluency and comprehension skills evolve together throughout every grade and subject in a student's academic life" (Sparks, 2012, p. 6). The CCSS "demand better analysis and argumentation skills, a greater emphasis on academic language, and greater attention to students building content knowledge and reading skills from independently tackling information text" (Neuman & Roskos, 2012, p. 207).

In the early elementary grades, the CCSS introduce a number of changes from current, individual states' standards (Berkin, 2012; International Reading Association, 2012; Neuman & Roskos, 2012). The most notable include the following:

- Explicit preparation to read informational text
- Reading materials that are substantively and meaningfully linked to content areas
- Use of more academic or technical vocabulary
- More informational writing

These four areas are the core instructional strategies described in this book. Specifically, we address the use of informational reading and writing resources as a way of (1) enriching and expanding the English language arts curriculum in the early elementary grades and (2) simultaneously providing instruction in other content areas. Because our work has involved integrating science-related informational text into kindergarten classes, we will use examples from that content area and grade level. However, the same ideas and strategies apply to other content areas (e.g., social studies) and to elementary grades beyond kindergarten.

## OVERVIEW OF CHAPTERS

In Chapter 1, we begin with an overview of reading as the top priority in the early grades. We discuss the characteristics of narrative and fictional texts, and we outline reasons for the predominance of narrative fiction. We then discuss what children learn *uniquely* from informational text and review the serious consequences that follow from an early narrow literacy focus on fictional genres.

In Chapter 2, we consider the educator arguments that young children learn most easily through narrative and that informational or expository text is too difficult and should be introduced later. We provide evidence to show that those arguments are erroneous; young children can *comprehend* informational text, even after a single read-aloud experience, and can *accurately retell* the text's content.

We examine, in Chapter 3, the concern that young children do not find informational books interesting. We then present evidence showing that, in fact, young children find informational texts *extremely interesting* and, moreover, that there is no difference between girls and boys in their enjoyment of these texts.

In Chapter 4, we consider criteria that educators can apply when deciding which informational books to use in their classrooms. We examine issues of accuracy in various types of informational texts, children's ability to distinguish fact from fiction—a matter that comes into play in hybrid texts that include both informational and fictional content—and consider the role of images as well as issues of equity.

Next, in Chapter 5, we review the evidence on the vital role of shared reading in literacy development and discuss research-based strategies that promote young children's literacy. We also present interactive book-reading strategies that are appropriate to use with informational genres and that can be effectively implemented during read-alouds in order to support children's development of literacy and content knowledge.

In Chapter 6, we focus on pairing informational texts in subject-area disciplines with writing specific to those content areas. After first reviewing the role that writing plays in supporting reading, we discuss how writing activities can be used to document inquiry. We present numerous examples that demonstrate kindergarteners' informational writing associated with book-reading and inquiry activities and that represent a wide range of children's abilities.

Finally, in Chapter 7 we discuss children's access to informational books at home and consider why and how regular parent-child reading and conversations around these books play important roles in addressing children's thirst for new knowledge. We argue for the use of strategies that, when implemented both at home and school, can serve as common tools for parents and teachers to enrich and provide continuity in children's learning experiences. Also, we present examples of ways that educators can guide and support parents' efforts to read and discuss informational books with their children.

Our hope is that this book shows how you can incorporate informational books in your reading and English language arts curriculum, while at the same time providing rich opportunities for your students to learn crucial subject areas that have typically been underserved (e.g., science, social studies, informational and subject-specific writing). In doing so, we also address how you can realistically address the CCSS in the early grades, in addition to meeting the best practices that are recommended for teaching science (National Research Council, 2007, 2012) and social studies (National Council for the Social Studies, 2012b).

---

**PAUSE TO REFLECT**

1. What do the authors discuss in this Introduction that:
   a. surprises you: points that you had never considered?
   b. irritates you: ideas with which you disagree?
   c. pleases you: positions that you have always held?

2. What questions do you have about informational texts and young children before you begin reading this book? What do you look forward to reading more about?

3. What teaching practices or pedagogical beliefs do you hold that might be in conflict with the purposes of this book? How might your current practice be informed?

---

## HIGHLY RECOMMENDED READING

International Reading Association Common Core State Standards Committee. (2012). *Literacy implementation guidance for the ELA Common Core State Standards* [White paper]. Washington, DC: Author. Retrieved from http://www.reading.org/Libraries/association-documents/ira_ccss_guidelines.pdf

# English Language Arts in the Early Years of School

*Priorities and Consequences*

**D**eveloping children's reading skills is viewed as the greatest instructional priority during the early years of elementary school. After decades of concern about low student achievement, the current near-exclusive emphasis on early literacy is based on the belief that reading skills form the foundation for success in other content areas, and therefore children with strong early literacy skills are well prepared for learning all other academic subjects. Kindergarten and first-grade teachers are held accountable for their students' reading scores, and parents are bombarded with messages about the importance and benefits of reading with their children.

Young children's experiences with print, both at home and at school, generally involve picture books with fictional stories.

Even before formal instruction in reading begins, shared book reading between children and parents or other family members creates a context for children to learn reading-related routines and to develop an awareness of how print is used and what it tells us. For example, with help from adults, children gradually become familiar with conventional reading behaviors, such as holding the book, opening at the first page, and turning the pages from front to back. Children also learn about the conventions of print. For instance, they come to understand that we read words in English from left to right and from top to bottom, and that spoken words are represented by sets of letters that are grouped together to form words and sentences.

Over time, as they continue reading picture books, children develop more skills that are central to comprehending written language: They recognize a book's pictures are related to the text, and therefore knowledge gained from one can be used to understand the other. They learn that information on one page is linked to that on previous and subsequent pages, and that together the pages tell a story or build on a theme. Through features such as repetition of words or predictable patterns of events, children anticipate events or phrases that come later in the story. From these experiences, children learn they can expect to be able to make inferences about a book's content to predict what may come next. In addition, through talking about books, children learn to summarize and synthesize information, grasp the importance of sequencing, and come to distinguish important details from those in the background (Paris & Paris, 2003). Critical thinking and communication skills that are necessary for school, work, and successful living in general are grounded in children's early reading experiences with adults. Fortunately, reading picture books is not just tremendously beneficial—apparently without exception, children find picture books enjoyable, engaging, and entertaining. It is not surprising, then, that picture books play an essential part in early literacy instruction.

Picture books come in a variety of genres, or styles, including *narrative* (story based) and *expository* (or strictly informational). Narrative and informational books have different structures and features, but both types of texts are important to literacy instruction. As we discuss in this book, familiarity with both genres contributes to children developing different types of skills and ways of understanding and learning about the world. We explain what we mean by this by discussing fictional narratives, and then informational books, in the next sections.

## FICTIONAL NARRATIVE PICTURE BOOKS

Fictional narrative books are written to primarily entertain by telling a story. They are constructed around a set of characters (people, animals, or even machines, toys, or other objects) who enact a sequential and more-or-less predictable plot. The content may be either realistic or wholly fanciful; it may also include factual information within the fictional plot. The characters (even the nonhuman ones are portrayed with human qualities) establish relationships among themselves. They have feelings, intentions, and goals or desires. They experience particular outcomes as a result of their actions, often learning a lesson along the way. For example, a train may get tired of staying on the railroad tracks and decide to leave them to play in the fields, only to learn that it is a mistake to "go off the rails," as in the Golden Book *Tootle* (Crampton, 1945). Or a train may be content with her lot in life only to face a crisis of confidence, as occurs in *The Little Engine That Could* (Piper, 1976):

> The little train rumbled over the tracks. She was a happy little train for she had just a jolly load to carry. Her cars were filled with good things for boys and girls. . . . The little train was carrying all these wonderful things to the little boys and girls on the other side of the mountain. She putted along merrily. Then all of a sudden she stopped with a jerk. She simply could not go another inch. She tried and tried but her wheels would not turn.

In addition to the sequential story, other typical features of narrative texts for young children include the use of past tense or "real time" verbs; everyday, nontechnical vocabulary.

Conventional phrases such as the opening "once upon a time . . ." and the ending " . . . they lived happily ever after" are commonly used. Pictures reinforce the ideas presented in the text or help the reader fill in details beyond the actual words (Donovan & Smolkin, 2002).

Let's consider more specifically how several of these features are present in the story structure, language, and the illustrations of *The Little Engine That Could*. The story unfolds in a sequence of events: The initiating event—the Little Engine breaking down— is followed first by her despair and then by her attempts to solve the problem (e.g., looking for help from other engines). These efforts lead eventually to a successful outcome and a newfound sense of confidence as the Little Engine manages to deliver her load as expected. The story's moral (*"I think I can, I think I can"*) is one of building confidence—believing in oneself and being successful through hard work, perseverance, and effort. The moral develops as the resolution to the problem emerges and continues to be highlighted until the end of the story, when a successful solution is achieved (*"I thought I could. I thought I could . . ."*).

Past tense is used throughout the book, and the vocabulary is straightforward, without complex terms or events that young children might not be familiar with. Encounters with words like "rumbled," that may not yet be part of a young child's vocabulary (cf., Chall & Dale, 1995), are unlikely to interfere with comprehension because they occur in a simple, familiar context (in terms of both the predictability of the story structure and children's general familiarity with the issues embedded in the plot). Children draw from this familiar framework to infer that the meaning of "rumbled" has something to do with the way the train moved "happily" along the tracks.

The illustrations in *The Little Engine That Could* aid children's comprehension by focusing attention on important aspects of the story, supporting and reinforcing the messages presented in the written text. In the excerpt reproduced here (see Figure 1.1), the Little Engine is drawn with a sad face,

| **Figure 1.1** | Illustration From *The Little Engine That Could* |

What were all those good little boys and girls on the other side of the mountain going to do without the wonderful toys to play with and the good food to eat?

*Source*: Piper (1976).

which reflects the disappointment she felt after her engine failed and her "wheels would not turn." The engine's expression also captures her concern for the recipients (the "good little boys and girls on the other side of the mountain") of her "jolly load," who would not receive the presents (toys, dolls, a baby elephant, and "the funniest little toy clown you ever saw") if the engine could not get over the mountain. The little bear's facial expression and gesturing also reflect concern about the toys' fate, whereas the clown shows several cues (looking along the other tracks, waving a flag in anticipation) for what comes next in the story (perhaps help from a new engine that is arriving on the scene). These illustrations encourage children to feel the emotions described in the story and make personal connections to the characters and their circumstances.

## INFORMATIONAL PICTURE BOOKS

Unlike fictional books, informational texts for young children do not rely on telling a story laden with characters and emotion. Instead, the goal is to communicate information about facts (e.g., uses of microscopes), processes (e.g., how a flower grows), or a sequence of procedures and techniques for achieving an outcome (e.g., how to bake cornbread).

The following excerpt from *Simple Machines* (Fowler, 2001, pp. 3–7), a trade book intended for children in Grades K–2, illustrates several of the common features of information books:

> We use machines (muh-SHEENS) every day. Machines help make our lives easier. Some machines, such as lawn mowers and vacuum (VAK-yoom) cleaners have many parts. Other machines have few parts. They are called simple machines. Levers, inclined planes, wheels and axles (AK-suls), and pulleys are four kinds of simple machines.

As we see here, informational books communicate accurate knowledge to the reader through structures that describe, compare and contrast, and classify. They may also explain cause-and-effect relations and if-then sequences (Duke & Kays, 1998). Unlike with a story, where the sequence of events in time is crucial for it to make sense, the content in informational texts does not necessarily have to be presented in a particular order. For instance, the simple machines book could equally well proceed to discuss levers or inclined planes next. There are, of course, some instances when the sequence in time is important even in informational text, such as passages recounting historical events, life cycles, or procedures.

Rather than relying on characters, informational books refer to a topic or theme throughout as a way of connecting one part of the text with the next, therefore providing cohesion and continuity for the reader. In this excerpt, the topic, *machines,* is used several times to help the reader maintain focus and connect with the information presented in each sentence. Present tense verbs and forms of the verbs *to have* and *to be* are standard features of informational books (Duke & Kays, 1998), as shown in the excerpt from *Simple Machines.* The language is enriched with technical terms (e.g., levers, inclined planes, axles, pulleys) and topics (e.g., ways to categorize machines) that are not likely to be part of children's routine conversations at home or school (De Temple & Snow, 2003; Pappas, 1993, 2006; Yopp & Yopp, 2000). The vocabulary of informational texts is typically more advanced than the everyday, common-sense vocabulary encountered in fiction-oriented picture books.

Just like fictional picture books, informational texts for young children are full of illustrations (including photographs or drawings) that show content presented in the book, such as types of traditional clothing worn in different countries, astronauts working in space, or what baby animals look like compared to their mothers. The graphic content of informational books is realistic and may include photographs, drawings, maps, tables, or diagrams. These visuals help young readers to

- construct literal descriptions of the content (e.g., see what the first American flag looked like);
- make predictions about the information covered in the text (e.g., what tragedy may strike a fisherman who is out on the ocean in his canoe when a storm strikes); or
- monitor their knowledge or realize that they are adding new information to what they already know about a topic (e.g., realize that not all birds use their wings to fly; Norman, 2010).

Several characteristics of informational texts for young children can be seen in Figure 1.2, which is an excerpt about the Hubble Space Telescope. Alongside the text is a National Aeronautic and Space Administration (NASA) photograph of

**Figure 1.2**    Informational Text: "The Hubble Telescope"

The Hubble telescope is in space, away from the Earth's atmosphere.

The Hubble telescope is a tool that scientists use.

It helps them learn about stars and planets that are far away from the Earth.

*Source:* Image from NASA (http://spaceflight.nasa.gov/gallery/images/shuttle/sts-103/html/sts103_726_081.html).

the Hubble orbiting the Earth. This photo illustrates information in the first sentence of the text—*The Hubble telescope is in space, away from the Earth's atmosphere*—and therefore helps children understand the sentence. This short text also includes many of the features that are typical of information genres. The text uses only the present tense (use, helps, learn, is, are), and every sentence includes existential verbs (is, are). The vocabulary includes several technical terms (atmosphere, telescope, planets) that are not likely to be familiar to children in the early elementary grades (Spache, 1978).

Repetition of the main topic—"the Hubble telescope"—within the short passage provides a coherent framework for the reader. Also, information that the Hubble is a tool far away from the Earth is given at both the beginning and the end of the passage as a way of helping the reader understand that the telescope is distant in order to help scientists learn about far-away objects.

Unlike fiction, the text is not based on characters and their experiences. Instead, coherence, meaning-making, and engagement with it develop as the reader grasps and makes sense of the knowledge contained in the text. It is this very act of purposeful meaning-making that fulfills children's natural curiosity about the world and makes informational texts highly interesting and motivating. Experiences with expository texts inform and cultivate readers' interests while at the same time fueling their ongoing thirst for knowledge (Alexander, 1997).

## THE PREDOMINANCE OF NARRATIVE TEXT

Narrative and informational texts have different structures and features, and students need to comprehend each well (National Council of Teachers of English [NCTE] and International Reading Association [IRA], 1996). By fourth grade, children are expected to be able to read and understand both genres well; this includes expecting students to learn from textbooks in subjects such as science and social studies. However, fictional and informational texts have not been given equal weight in the early years of school—a practice the Common Core State Standards (National Governors Association [NGA] & Council of Chief State School Officers [CCSSO], 2010) seek to change.

Beginning at preschool, children receive many more experiences with narrative than with informational texts (Pentimonti, Zucker, &, Justice, 2011; Price, Bradley, & Smith, 2012). This trend continues in kindergarten and the early grades, where instruction is still heavily focused on narrative genres (Yopp & Yopp, 2012). It is estimated that in first grade, children spend less than 3.6 minutes per day with informational text—much too little time for them to learn from and learn about this genre (Duke, 2000). Only a small proportion of books read aloud by PK–Grade 3 teachers are informational—8% in a recent study (Yopp & Yopp, 2012). During 1970–2000, less than one quarter of the content of elementary grade basal readers was informational (Kamil & Bernhardt, 2004). The amount of informational text contained in basal readers has increased in recent years, along with their overall use (Moss, 2008; Ness, 2011). However, the general distribution of informational texts relative to narrative texts in basal readers does not yet meet the 2009 National Assessment of Educational Progress recommendations (Moss, 2008), which are endorsed by the Common Core State Standards (NGA & CCSSO, 2010).

## Rationales for the Predominance of Fiction

One argument for the predominance of fiction asserts that children are predisposed to learning from stories, because the capacity for storylike thinking and information processing is an essential part of being human (McClure & Zitlow, 1991; Wells, 1985). Therefore, the argument goes, instruction is likely to be most successful when content is taught within stories.

A related argument claims that some subjects (e.g., math, science) and discipline-specific ways of learning about the world (e.g., scientific inquiry) are, by their nature, not story-shaped and so young children find them difficult and uninteresting. Therefore, using books without stories, such as informational texts, to teach these subjects contributes to children losing attention and becoming bored. Consequently, the argument goes, instruction in the early years of school should be organized within stories, so as to encourage student interest and promote meaningful learning, even in subjects such as math and science. Teachers, it is claimed, should be storytellers, who view and organize instruction around telling good stories, rather than achieving a list of objectives (Egan, 1988).

Consistent with these positions, narrative picture books like Eric Carle's (1987) *The Very Hungry Caterpillar* are frequently used to teach young children about science topics such as the life cycle of butterflies. The book provides information about how an egg changes to a caterpillar, which ultimately becomes a butterfly, but it also contains a number of fanciful inaccuracies, such as that caterpillars eat lollipops, pickles, and cherry pie. Therefore, despite the book's immense entertainment value, it can cause young children to develop significant misconceptions, or inaccurate beliefs, about the diet and feeding habits of caterpillars. When we have observed teachers reading this book, we have seen that usually the main or only objective is for children to enjoy the story. Little attention is paid to whether the children learn any of the accurate science content woven skillfully throughout the story, or if they understand that the fanciful parts are not true to life.

Even when narrative texts include generous descriptions of accurate, subject-specific information (as in the case for the science content embedded in *The Magic School Bus* series), they continue to strengthen the readers' skills in reading narratives while providing few insights into how to navigate the language and structure of informational genres. We discuss the kinds of knowledge that young children construct from reading these types of "mixed" (i.e., narrative and information) texts in Chapter 4.

Does research evidence support the rationales for focusing almost exclusively on reading fictional books in the earliest grades? Some (but not all) research shows that older elementary-grade students find narrative text easier to understand than informational text; for example, a study suggests that third graders learn more science content when the information is presented as a story (Leal, 1994). However, to interpret this finding, we should consider that by third grade these children most likely have had disproportionally fewer experiences with informational texts both at home and in school (because children are typically expected to read such texts only from fourth grade on). Therefore, it is likely that children's comprehension skills for informational texts had not been sufficiently developed by third grade, which would explain the research favoring fiction. Instead of justifying the focus on fiction in the early grades, this research may be revealing a consequence of the practice of relying on narrative!

Other research has run counter to the notion that storied formats facilitate the comprehension of information. For instance, Maria and Junge (1994) noted that the fantasy elements of mixed texts may interfere with the learning of informational ideas because children, who have had more experiences and familiarity with fiction, focus on the details of the story and ignore the informational content. More recent evidence supports this point and highlights a number of concerns associated with "storybook" science texts. Groups of fourth graders who read about the same science content in either fictional narrative or informational texts differed with respect to the number and accuracy of science concepts they remembered. Even though children could retell more when the science content was embedded in fictional narrative, they had better and more accurate retellings of the main science concepts when they were learned from informational texts. Also, it is particularly disconcerting that the children who read the fictional narrative had twice as many misconceptions about the science concepts presented in the book compared with children who read the expository text (Cervetti, Bravo, Hiebert, & Pierson, 2009).

Research with children in the early years of school is currently on the rise. It is noteworthy that studies conducted in a variety of contexts (e.g., developmental labs as well as school and family settings) report that preschool and kindergarten children derive many benefits from shared (adult-child) readings of informational books. That is, preschoolers not only learn factual content from picture books, but also are able to apply that knowledge to interpret real-world situations (Ganea, Ma, & DeLoache, 2011). Of interest, iconicity, or the level of realistic representation in pictures, influences the extent to which children transfer the information to new situations. The more realistic the book's picture, the greater the transfer (e.g., Ganea, Pickard & DeLoache, 2008)—a finding that supports the value of informational texts for children's learning about the world. This finding may also explain another finding: that children are better able to transfer solutions to problems when they have learned about them in stories with real people rather than in stories with fantasy characters (Richert & Smith, 2011). Though this research does not address the many benefits that children derive from experiences with diverse texts (fictional, informational, and mixed types), it does call attention to the need to broaden the scope of books children read and to consider the multiple benefits of diverse genres for children's learning and motivation.

Fictional narrative does play a critical role in children's early learning. However, its heavy predominance in the early elementary grades builds and reinforces a narrow set of skills that are insufficient for the comprehension of the non-narrative, informational texts that children will encounter in later grades when they begin instruction in other disciplines. Although children who are familiar with fictional stories are also much better at understanding novel fictional texts, the skills they use are not necessarily helpful when they are faced with expository texts (Hall, Sabey, & McLellan, 2005). There is virtually no evidence to support the notion that young children are predisposed to learn from narrative and are therefore more interested in it. Moreover, there are compelling arguments that information-oriented texts are motivating and support children's intrinsic needs for learning about and understanding the world (Alexander, 1997). In conclusion, findings from recent research summarized briefly here raise concerns about the early and nearly exclusive reliance on fiction and its role in children's motivation and learning.

## UNINTENDED CONSEQUENCES OF FICTION-ONLY CURRICULA

Learning from text is shaped not only by the quality of ideas and illustrations but also by the text's features and structure (Teale, 2003). Children's awareness of different types of text and their underlying structures (e.g., fictional, informational, or mixed genres) plays a major role in the breadth and depth of knowledge that they construct during reading. It follows that the disproportionate attention to narrative texts strengthens skills that are essential for that genre but neglects the development of other skills necessary to read informational text. Thin opportunities to learn from informational texts in the early grades constrain children's ability to process and enjoy this type of text because they lack experiences with the frameworks typical for this genre. Therefore, even though both narrative and informational texts may contain unfamiliar information, they are not equally difficult for children who have read only narrative genres and are familiar with this class of texts. Waiting until third or fourth grade to introduce informational text typically leads to children having well-developed knowledge structures, skills, and social knowledge that enable them to comprehend events described in narrative while being ill prepared for learning from informational text.

The ability to read and understand informational texts in content areas such as science and social studies requires more than general competencies for processing expository text. There is no evidence in support of the assumption that generic or all-purpose literacy skills are easily transferrable from storied to informational texts and then successfully used to make meaning from reading in content areas unfamiliar to readers—young children and adults alike. In addition to needing sufficiently developed frameworks for this type of text, children need prior discipline-specific background and vocabulary knowledge to move beyond the literal, surface features of the reading and make meaningful linkages with the new ideas in informational texts (Best, Floyd, & McNamara, 2008; Hiebert & Cervetti, 2011; Hirsch, 2006). Readers who integrate their prior relevant knowledge with the new information learned during reading are better able to recall the information, use it to learn new material, and apply it to solve problems (Wolfe & Woodwyk, 2010).

Integrating literacy activities in content area instruction (e.g., science) should involve more than reading books such as

*The Very Hungry Caterpillar* (even though it and others like it are wonderful books—for a different purpose) to teach about the butterfly life cycle. Rather, instruction should afford opportunities for learning from high-quality, informationally accurate texts and using discipline-appropriate reading strategies and writing resources to represent learning. For instance, in a journal or notebook, children can use a variety of strategies (writing, drawing, pasting photographs) to represent both their prior and new knowledge. They can document their questions, record the new concepts that they have learned, show how they can apply them, and summarize conclusions. The inclusion of writing activities in the context of learning from informational texts during content-area instruction provides an authentic setting for the development of literacy skills while highlighting the value of writing as an important form of communication (Patrick, Mantzicopoulos, & Samarapungavan, 2009b). We elaborate on this point in Chapter 6.

## The Costs of Relying on Fiction

All in all, the reliance on fictional narrative books to teach topics in other content areas comes with a number of costs.

1. The emphasis on skills and strategies that are specific to one class of texts (e.g., fiction) disregards the genres, conventions, and ultimately the integrity of individual disciplines (e.g., literature, science) and does not help children construct accurate conceptions of them.

2. Misconceptions, or inaccuracies, are likely to develop or become reinforced (if children already hold them) when factual content is intertwined with fiction because young children may not be able to distinguish between what is true in the book and what is not (see also Chapter 4). They may conclude, for example, that although very hungry caterpillars hatch from eggs and

transform into a chrysalis, they also feast on cherry pie and chocolate cake. In the context of the book reading, and without explicit instruction, all these activities may sound equally plausible to young children.

3. The lack of experiences with informational texts in the early grades does not build either the background knowledge or the genre-specific skills that children need for reading science and social studies texts in later grades. Reading is more than knowing what the words say and mean; it also involves understanding the words' meanings in relation to each other and in the context of the particular discipline. For example, "a long time" in history does not mean the same as "a long time" in earth science. Because language provides the tools for thinking, deficits in discipline-specific language inevitably make it difficult for children to gain access to the knowledge that this language expresses (i.e., content knowledge) and to understand the discipline that it represents (Moje, 2008; Shanahan & Shanahan, 2008). For example, events in history are recorded and understood differently than physics-related phenomena and are therefore represented through language differently. Without a foundation of the vocabulary and linguistic conventions used in a field of study, people cannot develop adequate views of that field. This may sound like a consideration most relevant for later grade levels, but reading of good, appropriate informational texts in the early grades can lay a stronger base for interacting with these features later.

4. When children experience only fiction, it is likely to stifle their interest and motivation both for reading informational books and for engaging with the content areas. For example, many books that contain science content "jazz up" the science by adding magical or fantasy elements (e.g., the school bus children are riding on shrinks so they can travel throughout the inner systems

of a living person). Children may come to believe that these fantasy elements are what make science exciting, rather than appreciating the wonder of the real world (e.g., the amazingly elaborate structures and processes at work inside of us). After having developed an expectation, over years, that science involves fantasy, children encountering a "different kind" of science book (i.e., an expository one) may find it rather mundane. However, if children develop a realistic notion, early, of what science is and their instruction addresses their natural curiosity and fascination with the world, children will likely not be set up for later disappointment when they are expected to be learning science as a required component of the curriculum.

In conclusion, the early and targeted engagement with fiction supports and hones the development of skills that are fundamental to reading fictional genres. Conversely, insufficient experience with informational texts deprives children of opportunities to develop skills that are essential for comprehending and learning from nonfictional, expository genres. Balancing this lopsided pattern of instructional choices is crucial to avoid the potentially far-reaching, unwelcome consequences for both children's reading competencies and their subject-specific learning.

Reading informational books and developing competence in the use of inscriptional resources (e.g., constructing graphs, using written language, pictures, or drawings to record observations and events) provide instructional entry points to incorporating important disciplines, such as science and social studies, into the curriculum. Having said this, let us be clear that engagement with informational texts alone cannot fill the void of content-area instruction in the early years of school. However, the purposeful inclusion of informational resources in the curriculum would maintain the early focus on reading and language arts and make it more balanced in terms of genres while simultaneously addressing some standards for the other content areas. Currently this is far from the norm. We elaborate on how teachers can accomplish this, and provide examples from kindergarten science classes, in the chapters that follow.

## CHAPTER 1 APPLICATIONS FOR PRACTICE

### Try-It-On Activities

The following suggested activities require that you try out ideas presented in this chapter in your classroom.

1. Make a list of the high-quality informational texts that you use in your instruction. What does the list reflect in terms of the points made in Chapter 1?

2. Review narrative books that you especially promote in your classroom, and evaluate them in terms of the misconceptions (science-related as well as other disciplines) that might be communicated or reinforced.

## FOR DISCUSSION AND REFLECTION

1. What instructional decisions need to be made when a narrative book (e.g., *The Very Hungry Caterpillar*) presents information? What are potential opportunities and challenges when books combine narrative with informational text? Can you provide an example of such a book from your own practice?

2. What are the "intended" consequences of a fiction-only curriculum? The authors propose a number of unintended consequences, but what is a fiction-only curriculum supposed to advocate and teach? Can these goals still be accomplished using some expository nonfiction books in addition to using fiction?

## HIGHLY RECOMMENDED WEBSITES FOR LOCATING AWARD-WINNING INFORMATIONAL TEXTS

National Council of Teachers of English Orbis Pictus Award for Outstanding Nonfiction for Children: http://www.ncte.org/awards/orbispictus

International Reading Association's Children's and Young Adult's Book Award http://www.reading.org/Resources/Awardsand Grants/childrens_ira.aspx

# 2

# Do Young Children Find Informational Books Hard to Understand?

I n the previous chapter, we discussed the major reasons for why children in the early elementary grades usually have few experiences with informational books: Stories are considered fun and easy for young children to understand, whereas informational books are believed to be too difficult (Donovan & Smolkin, 2001). The research evidence shows, however, that this concern is unfounded. In this chapter, we address what young children do learn and remember from informational books, and we suggest why many children struggle with informational texts. We also present examples from children's family conversations and our work with students in kindergarten science classrooms.

**PAUSE TO REFLECT**

1. Which concerns do you hold about informational books for young children?

2. How might your concerns be reflected in your practice?

3. Do you read informational books as frequently as narrative books?

4. Are you more interested in narrative books than informational books for young children?

5. What does your classroom library say about the choices your students have?

6. Does your school library allow young children the same access to informational books as it does to fictional books?

## EASING INTO INFORMATIONAL GENRES THROUGH NARRATIVE: FACT AND FICTION

In Chapter 1, we summarized arguments suggesting that young children find it easy to understand narratives because of both experiences in their environment and their innate abilities. The same reasons—nature and nurture—also explain why children struggle with content communicated in expository texts.

One perspective claims that because children have a natural tendency to organize their thoughts and memories as narratives, they will find informational content too dull, too difficult to process, and not enjoyable. A similar viewpoint holds that the structure and vocabulary of narrative are not as complex as that of informational text, therefore young children learn narrative content easily but need formal training to understand informational text (Graesser, Golding, & Long, 1991). Although these perspectives may sound reasonable, research shows clearly that *they are not accurate.* For example, later in this chapter we discuss how these views about informational books are contradicted by practices in other countries, where different educational beliefs and practices lead to informational books being heavily favored over fiction.

## The Role of Narrative
## in Remembering Everyday Events

Narrative is easy to comprehend because that is how we connect sequences of events that we experience and talk about in daily life. From a very early age, children are immersed in a social world, where they learn and remember experiences through the telling of stories (Graesser et al., 1991). Indeed, narrative is fundamental to developing episodic memory—a type of memory that involves organizing, storing, and recalling circumstances and experiences that we have observed or have actively participated in (Nelson & Fivush, 2004). Episodic memory is a valuable and uniquely human capacity that is rooted in daily social interactions. It is from these interactions that children make sense of the past; they note and remember what the events were, when and where they took place, who the participants were, and what their actions, intentions, and feelings were.

With the growth of language skills, children become increasingly able to remember and talk about events they have experienced themselves, such as a trip to the zoo, a visit to the doctor's office, or their daily school activities (DeMarie, Norman, & Abshier, 2000; Murachver, Pipe, Gordon, Owens, & Fivush, 1996; Tessler & Nelson, 1994). Shared parent-child reminiscing about the past helps children to understand events and create memories that are coherent and sequenced accurately, and it enables children to think about different points in time, shifting their thoughts from the present to the past and back again. Parents, through their use of interpretive comments, prompts, and cues, highlight key features of specific occasions and help children revisit the past and rethink, reorganize, and reframe their knowledge about events and themselves (Nelson & Fivush, 2004). Therefore, narrative is an invaluable resource that allows humans to access, share, or organize their memories.

In the following excerpt, we show how a parent uses prompts to help her child recall a previous doctor's visit and then use that memory to put another child's negative statement into perspective. Ultimately, the child readjusts her expectations and overall perceptions of the experience.

**Mom:**     *Tomorrow after school we have to see Dr. Araki for your booster shots.*

**Denise:**  *Lane said that going to the doctor is scary.*

**Mom:**     *What do you think?*

**Denise:**  *Well, Dr. Araki gave me my shot last time we were there.*

**Mom:**     *And was that scary?*

**Denise:**  *Only a little bit.*

**Mom:**     *What part of it was a little bit scary?*

**Denise:**  *'Cause I thought it would hurt, but you told me it wouldn't.*

**Mom:**     *And did it?*

**Denise:**  *Not really. It didn't hurt.*

**Mom:**     *What did it feel like?*

**Denise:**  *Um, like a little pinch, a tiny one. And then I even got a sticker for being so good.*

In the following two excerpts, we illustrate conversations between two children, Dima and Drake, and their mothers. The two mothers use prompts and focusing statements differently to support their child's memory of the pilgrim story that was discussed that day in Mrs. Ateur's class.

*Dima and His Mother*

**Dima:**  *And Mrs. Ateur told us about pilgrims today!*

**Mom:**   *Tell me, I can't wait to hear.*

**Dima:**  *Well, there were the pilgrims and they had a feast with the Indians.*

**Mom:**   *Where did the pilgrims come from?*

**Dima:** *And they came from England and then . . . from there they went to the . . . um . . . comoach (Dima's nonsense word) . . . to the comoach.*

**Mom:** *What is the comoach again?*

**Dima:** *It's a place here in America, mommy, it's where they went. It's on the map. Mrs. Ateur showed us on the map where they went.*

**Mom:** *Here, in the United States? Hm . . . where? Do you want to bring the globe and show me too?*

**Dima:** *OK (brings the globe, then twists the globe on its axis) . . . um . . . Here it is . . . Europe . . . they came from England. Here it is! I found it.*

**Mom:** *Show me, where?*

**Dima:** *Here (pointing to England). See?*

**Mom:** *Yes. What is this country in Europe called?*

**Dima:** *Um . . . it says it here, and I knew it before. They came from, from, from England! That's where they came from (keeps pointing on the globe). And then they went all the way to over . . . over . . . here (shows the coast of the United States). They came to another place.*

**Mom:** *Where is this place?*

**Dima:** *I don't see what it's called here (pointing to the globe), but it was their NEW country. They all landed in Virginia first. They came from one England to the new world.*

**Mom:** *And the new world? Did it have a name?*

**Dima:** *It was called America. And they made a place called Jamestown and also Plymouth.*

**Mom:** *OK, I see. From England, they came to America and settled in Virginia. And built Jamestown? Now, how does the story go that Mrs. Ateur told? First, the pilgrims . . .*

**Dima:** *Well, at first, they came from Europe, the pilgrims. England is where that they lived at first. That was their first country.*

*And then, they came all the way, over the ocean, to America. See, Mommy? (shows on the globe) And they came to Virginia first, right here, see? (shows on the globe) And they liked it a lot. And they got good yummy stuff to eat, like fish and eels. Well, not at first, it was hard.*

**Mom:**    *Why was it hard?*

**Dima:**   *They had to find food and shelter. But then the Indians helped them and they became friends with them. And they learned to farm. And they caught yummy fish and eels. And they had a feast.*

*Drake and His Mother*

**Mom:**    *What did you learn in school today?*

**Drake:**  *The pilgrims had a feast!*

**Mom:**    *OK, that's interesting. And what happened at the feast?*

**Drake:**  *With the Indians. They met the chief, he was called . . . Squanto and he spoke a little English. So he talked to them in his little English.*

**Mom:**    *Aha . . . and then?*

**Drake:**  *Then they lived happily ever after!*

**Mom:**    *That's good. And what else did you do at school today?*

---

**PAUSE AND REFLECT**

1. After reading these two excerpts, think about how each mother's responses to her son shapes his understanding.
2. What does each mother do throughout her child's narrative to help him build a cohesive, versus a disjointed, understanding of the lesson?
3. What is each child likely to remember about the pilgrim lesson?

## Children's Early Interest in Information

Our ability to understand narratives begins early in life. As we noted in the previous section, narrative is central to mentally representing, organizing, and remembering situations and events. It also has parallels with the language and characteristics of storied texts. Because of these parallels, it is generally assumed that young children find narrative stories enticing and their structure and overall language demands easy to process. Although correct, *this does not mean that children are strangers to exposition or that they find it unappealing or the language unmanageable.*

There is ample evidence that children are information seekers. They have a great deal of interest in events and phenomena that they cannot personally experience or explore in their immediate environment. For example, children initiate conversations in the course of everyday activities and ask many questions about the natural and technological world (Chouinard, 2007). As we discuss further in Chapter 7, children ask about such things as what causes clouds or rainbows or mountains to form, why rain falls, how the sun or stars "stay up" in the sky, how airplanes are made and how they fly, how babies are made, and why animals don't use words. These questions communicate children's interest and also that they are ready to gain new knowledge (Chin, Brown, & Bruce, 2002).

## Building Young Children's Content Knowledge With Narrative Versus Informational Genres

Research on memory as narrative focuses on sequences of events that involve particular people in specific settings. Events are remembered best when they are narrated in meaningfully connected sequences that include the characters and their goals, actions, and relationships and conclude with how an event is resolved or ends. However, narrative may not be the most appropriate framework for responding to children's information-seeking questions or helping them make sense of

expository or informational content. This is because the structure of exposition or informational text involves description,
comparison and contrast, an outline of procedures, and explanations of how things function—not features of narratives
(Weaver & Kintch, 1991).

When children ask their questions of people more knowledgeable than themselves, the conversations that follow guide
them in structuring, elaborating, and refining their knowledge. However, the flow of information in these adult-child
dialogues does not usually follow the narrative, storylike formats used to communicate and learn about personally experienced social events (e.g., a story learned in Mrs. Ateur's class,
a visit to grandma's, not getting along with friends).

During family conversations, parents sometimes do respond
to their children's requests for information by giving a familiar,
fictional answer, such as telling them that the reason there is
thunder is because the angels are bowling (Beals & Snow, 1994).
However, other parents answer children's information-seeking
questions in ways that parallel informational genres. This is
illustrated by the following family conversation in which
5-year-old twin daughters, LIO and IRI, talked with their
mother (MOT) and father (FAT) about seeing an anemone on a
preschool outing (Blum-Kulka & Snow, 1992, p. 212). Note how
the father, through his questions (e.g., *"What do you mean its
white part?"*), supports the girls in giving more accurate descriptions of what they observed and helps them explain the difference between poppies and anemones by prompting them to
recall information they were given by the guide.

**FAT:**   *Did you see any special animals? Did you find a grasshopper?*

**LIO:**   *Yes, I saw a grasshopper.*

**IRI:**   *They found an anemone?*

**FAT:**   *An anemone?*

**LIO:**   *I found it and I called Nili the teacher, and she said to everybody, "Look, look. I found an anemone."*

**FAT:**   *I haven't seen an anemone yet this year.*

**LIO:**  *I saw, I found the anemone.*

**FAT:**  *Already open?*

**LIO:**  *What? Yes, and we even saw its white part.*

**FAT:**  *What do you mean its white part?*

**LIO:**  *The white part inside the petals.*

**IRI:**  *No, there's also black.*

**LIO:**  *Yes, the stamens are black.*

**IRI:**  *I thought black.*

**LIO:**  *The white is altogether with . . .* (interrupted)

**FAT:**  *She said it's an anemone?*

**MOT:**  *There are anemones already?*

**FAT:**  *And what did the guides explain to you?*

**LIO:**  *I only have one guide.*

**FAT:**  *What did she tell you?*

**LIO:**  *She told us that you know it's an anemone because of its white part. Poppies are red without a white part.*

*Source:* Blum-Kulka & Snow (1992), p. 212.

## Diverse International Perspectives on Using Narrative and Informational Books in the Early School Years

Young children in American schools rarely experience informational books (Pentimonti et al., 2011). The almost exclusive focus on fiction is undoubtedly the reason why American fourth graders are significantly better at reading and understanding fictional stories than they are with informational texts (Mullis, Martin, Kennedy, & Foy, 2007). In many other countries, however, children are *not* better at reading fiction. For example, fourth graders in some countries (e.g., Scotland, Austria, Luxembourg) are equally skilled at reading fictional and informational texts, whereas others (e.g., in Singapore, Hong Kong, Indonesia) are better with informational text (Mullis et al., 2007). These differences reflect children's opportunities for reading different genres.

American teachers usually believe that informational books are too complex for young children to comprehend (Pentimonti et al., 2011). However, these beliefs are by no means universal. For example, Korean preschool teachers believe that an expository genre is easier for young children to understand and relate to than fiction, and that fantasy is particularly difficult (Y. Lee, Lee, Han, & Schickedanz, 2011). In line with this belief, Korean teachers in the early grades read mostly factual, informational texts to their students, and Korean children read and understand informational books better than fiction. Interestingly, the general patterns of how Korean and American preschoolers talk about either real or imaginary events also vary, depending on whether they typically experience informational or fantasy books.

## YOUNG CHILDREN'S LEARNING FROM INFORMATIONAL BOOKS

As we noted in Chapter 1, there has been a great deal of research about students' reading comprehension of narrative and expository texts spanning from the middle and upper elementary school grades to college. Unfortunately, these studies do not inform us about how and what *young* children learn from informational books. In the last decade, however, research in homes and in early school settings has begun to focus on informational genres.

Researchers are learning that young children benefit in important ways from reading informational texts. For example, preschoolers who read informational picture books develop specialized vocabulary and knowledge, can retell the concepts accurately, and can transfer, or use, knowledge learned in the books to describe similar objects or animals they encounter in the real world or to solve a simple problem

(Ganea et al., 2008, 2011; Leung, 2008; Richert & Smith, 2011). Children in the early-to-mid elementary grades (i.e., kindergarten to third grade) make strong gains in vocabulary and comprehension when their teachers incorporate the language and structure of informational books into their lessons (Hall et al., 2005; Mantzicopoulos, Patrick, & Samarapungavan, 2013; Purcell-Gates, Duke, & Martineau, 2007; Williams et al., 2005). Teachers may do this by engaging students in *authentic activities* that are consistent with the purpose of the text—to inform others about a particular topic.

## An Example of an Authentic Reading and Writing Activity

We illustrate how one teacher used an authentic activity and a related book about pond life, following her second-grade class's field trip to a nature preserve (Purcell-Gates et al., 2007). The teacher engaged her students in making a brochure that would answer the questions of other children who would visit the nature preserve in the future. Before the children began researching and writing their brochure, their teacher read them the following letter from Mr. Hernandez, the director of the nature preserve:

Dear Boys and Girls, I hope you enjoyed your visit to our pond. I enjoyed answering your many good questions about what lives in ponds. After you left, I thought about all of the other children who visit us and who also have many of the same questions. I thought it might be a good idea to have a brochure for them with answers to some of their questions. I am writing to ask if you would prepare a brochure like this. It could be called something like, "Questions and Answers About Pond Life." You could include some of your questions that you had before you visited us. If you write this, I will have many copies printed that we can put on the stand in the main office. That way, people can pick one up when they come or as they are leaving. I hope that you can do this for us. (p. 21)

Features that make this reading and writing activity an authentic one are that it

- was *meaningful* to the students' own experiences;
- had a *legitimate purpose*—there was a real reason why children should undertake the task;
- explicitly recognized the product (i.e., brochure) as a *tool* to provide information for others, rather than being a procedural exercise for only the teacher to read; and
- provided an opportunity for children to record *their* actual questions and document what they learned, using the informational book as a resource.

We will return later in this book to strategies for using informational books in the classroom (Chapter 5) and at home (Chapter 7). However, we presented this example here to emphasize that children learn about and from different genres when the instructional discourse and activities engage them in appropriate, genre-specific experiences with the text. This is in contrast to lessons and interactions that elicit narratives during discussions by focusing on children's personal responses to the text, without an emphasis on the text's content and the purpose for which it was written (Norris et al., 2008). For example, the teacher may have asked children if they have seen a pond before or how many of them like fishing in a pond. Although these questions may engage children's attention at the beginning of the story, targeted discussion about the science concepts and the content covered in the book is necessary for children to deepen their understanding.

## Kindergarteners Understand a Range of Informational Books

Most research on preliterate children's learning from and interest in expository genres, although limited, refers mostly to science- or technology-related books. The results are clear—young children benefit from reading expository text in terms of developing more advanced language and greater conceptual knowledge (Duke & Kays, 1998; Ford, Brickhouse, Lottero-Perdue, & Kittleson, 2006; Leung, 2008; Mohr, 2003; Richgels, 2002).

We have worked with kindergarteners, learning about what they understand from informational books on a range of science topics (Mantzicopoulos & Patrick, 2010). It's important to note that our students were not exceptionally advanced or privileged compared with other American kindergarteners. They were ethnically diverse (approximately one half were white and one fourth were Hispanic), came predominantly from low-income families, and attended schools where reading and mathematics test scores were consistently below the state average.

We assessed children's comprehension by reading excerpts from informational books individually to children and after each excerpt asking them to tell the text back to us. Each excerpt was printed on an 8.5-inch by 11-inch plate and contained text and a picture from a single commercially available informational science book targeted to kindergarteners. We chose books from a variety of sources, such as the following: (1) the lists of science books for young children published each year by the Children's Book Council and the National Science Teachers Association (NSTA, http://www.nsta.org/ostbc) and (2) publishers with a history of producing informational texts for young children (e.g., Abrams Learning Trends, Capstone Press, Children's Press, Dorling Kindersley, HarperCollins, National Geographic Society, Pearson Learning, Scholastic). We discuss considerations for choosing informational books in Chapter 4.

In Figure 2.1, we show an example of four of the plates we have developed; for copyright purposes, the photos shown are very similar but not identical to the ones we used. Two of the excerpts address biology—*Dolphins* (about a mother and baby dolphin) and *Fins, Wings, and Legs* (about structures that enable animals to move); one excerpt involves physical science—*What Is a Lever?* (about a seesaw or teeter-totter being a simple machine); and one involves earth and space science—*Light* (about the sun and Earth). The length and complexity of

**Figure 2.1**   Retelling Plates

**Dolphins**
by
Claire Robinson

At first, young dolphins live with their mothers.

The mother will feed and protect the baby.

Mothers teach the young dolphins many things.

In a year or two, the young dolphins leave to join a new school.

Photo from iStock. Text from Robinson (1999).

**Fins, Wings, and Legs**
by
Margaret Clyne and Rachel Griffiths

Many animals have legs.
Legs help animals move on land.
Legs help animals move in different ways.
A frog's legs help it hop far.
A cheetah's legs help it run fast.

Photos from iStock (top) and Thinkstock.com (bottom). Text from Clyne & Griffiths (2005).

**Light**
by
Monica Halpern

Most light on Earth comes from the sun, our nearest star.

The sun is our most important source of light and heat.

Without sunlight, Earth would be a cold, dark place. Nothing could live here.

Photo from Thinkstock.com. Text from Halpern (2002).

**What Is a Lever?**
by
Lloyd G. Douglas

A lever is a simple machine.
It is used to make work easier.
A lever moves up and down.
A seesaw is a lever. The seesaw moves up and down on a metal bar.

Photo from iStock. Text from Douglas (2002).

the text excerpts are comparable with each other; the number of characters, words, rare words, and sentences used are similar for each plate, as are the number and density of informational ideas in each excerpt.

With each excerpt, we began by showing just the picture to each child and asked what he or she thought the story might be about. We then guided the child through the listening part, as others have done (e.g., Duke & Kays, 1998; Morrow, 1990), by saying:

> *Let's find out what the author wrote about. Let's listen to the words in this story. The title is _____. Are you ready to listen to the story now? When I am done, I want you to tell the story back to me, as if you were telling it to a friend who has never heard it before. Ready to listen?*

At the end of the excerpt, we covered the text and asked the child to retell it by saying: *"Now it's your turn to be the story teller. Go ahead."* We could then compare the children's retellings with the original text, and so gain an understanding of the meaning that each child took away from each of the excerpts.

Importantly, the kindergarteners understood and could paraphrase the science texts' themes, even after just one reading. Across all four excerpts that we have shown here, approximately two thirds of the words the children used in their retellings were directly relevant to the text. Here is Sam's version of *Dolphins:*

**Sam:**   *They* [pointing to the dolphins] *live in the water.*

**Adult:**   *What else?*

**Sam:**   *Killer whales might eat him. Sharks can kill dolphins.*

**Adult:**   *What else was in this story?*

**Sam:**   *Some mom take* [sic] *care of him.*

Sam's statement *"Some mom take care of him"* reflects a thematically accurate understanding of *"The mother will protect the baby."* Further, he connected the information in the photograph with his prior knowledge (i.e., *"They live in the water"*), which he used to elaborate on the protection theme. Sam shared that dolphins are in danger from predators such as killer whales and sharks (i.e., *"Killer whales might eat him. Sharks can kill dolphins"*).

Sam's retelling was typical of retellings produced by young children following informational book readings (e.g., Moss, 1997). Other children's retelling also paraphrased the text accurately:

> *The dolphins teach the dolphins how to do things.*
>
> *The mama take* [sic] *care of them and the mom feeds them every day.*
>
> *Dolphins take care of their babies. They feed food to their babies. That's all.*
>
> *Dolphins. The moms do feed them and do lots of stuff and even guard the young dolphins and do all good stuff and even feed them all in one day and then they go to school.*

Many children, like Sam, added to the text read to them by weaving in their own background knowledge, prior experiences with the topic, or extensions from the accompanying picture. These additions tended to be relevant to the text and picture, as in these *Dolphins* examples:

> *They're swimming. They have fins. They have eyes.*
>
> *Theys* [sic] *got to find a new home so the baby dolphin can go to school.*
>
> *And, um, how will the mom find their babies when they are at school? Because all the dolphins are the same.*

The second biology text, *Fins, Wings, and Legs*, referred to animals' structure and function—a more mechanical topic than the relationship-oriented *Dolphins* text. The children were equally accurate in retelling each of these texts. Keisha's retelling of *Fins, Wings, and Legs* is typical:

**Keisha:**  *The legs are important for animals. And they help them to walk. And they have claws.*

**Adult:**  *Anything else?*

**Keisha:**  *No.*

Keisha's statement *"The legs are important for animals. And they help them to walk"* was a good thematic paraphrase of the text *"Legs help animals move on land,"* because *"walk"* is consistent with the textual theme that legs help animals move. Her retelling also included information that was not in the text (*"and they have claws"*), which reflects her prior knowledge that cats, of which the cheetah is one, have claws. Keisha's language reflects the language characteristic of informational text: she repeats the theme (*the legs . . . they help . . . they have . . .*) and uses timeless verbs (*help them to walk*).

Other children's thematically accurate retellings of this text include the following:

*Legs help us walk ways and run fast and frog legs help them hop far away.*

*The legs are important for animals. And they help them to walk.*

*The legs help things move on land. The frog's legs help the frog jump. The cheetah's legs help the cheetah run very fast.*

Some retellings were less accurate, but the children did make meaningful connections nevertheless. These included the following:

*Cheetahs are bad, bad, bad. Because they try to eat people.*

*The frog jump big and the, the cheetahs ran it and the frog jump over the cheetah to run away. And then they went that way [pointing].*

The children also showed good understanding of the excerpts from both the earth and space book *Light* and the physical science book *What Is a Lever?* In general, the kindergarteners' comprehension of the two books was comparable; they were equally accurate in retelling each of these texts. Typical examples include the following:

*Light*

*Light. Sun. Nothing live here. Dark. Cold.*

*There would be cold if it was dark all the time.*

*The sun is heat. If we don't have the sun it will be cold and darkness.*

*Without the sun it would be so dark, so no one could see and no one could live here.*

*No one could live there. It would be really cold and dark. That sunlight is important because it gives us all the heat we need. The Earth would be cold without it.*

*What Is a Lever?*

*It's a machine. You go up and down.*

*A seesaw moves on a metal bar. Levers makes [sic] it easier to work on.*

*A seesaw. You have to hold on to a metal bar that goes up and down.*

*It's about where you see a lever. It's a machine. It goes up and down. It has two metal bars. Like two machines.*

Just like they did with the biology texts, some children inserted additional information when they retold the excerpts on physical or earth science themes. Again, as we show in the following examples, their extensions were relevant to the texts' themes. It is particularly easy to recognize that children connected the *What Is a Lever?* text with their prior experiences playing on a seesaw or teeter-totter.

*Light*

*If we don't have any sunlight no one would live there on Earth because they'll have to live somewhere else because it be [sic] a cold dark place. God wouldn't let you be there.*

*Oh, water gets sun so the water can grow stuff. The water stays in the lake and the sun can warm the water up.*

*Nothing would live there. People would look for food. Light— you can see your shadow. You can look up in the sky.*

*What Is a Lever?*

*It goes to up and down each time. When it goes up the kids have fun.*

*That's how you make a seesaw. It's at the park and it's a play toy, but not one you can pick up. And that's all!*

### Children's Comprehension of Biology Versus Nonbiology Books

Our kindergarteners found some of the texts easier to paraphrase than others, even though the four excerpts were comparable in terms of text complexity. Children retold the two biology texts equally accurately, and the two physical/ earth science texts equally well; however, the biology texts were somewhat easier for them to paraphrase than the nonbiology texts. The children's retellings of the biology texts were longer and included more of the main ideas.

This difference in paraphrasing biology and nonbiology text is likely explained by the children's experiences. Children are better able to comprehend what they read (or have read to them) and learn new words when they can connect the new information with knowledge they already have about the topic (Dockrell, Braisby, & Best, 2007). Therefore, that children find the biology excerpts easier than the nonbiology ones reflects that they already know more about animals than they do about the physical world (Inagaki & Hatano, 2006), and that more informational science books available for young children are about the life sciences than any other type of science (Ford, 2006).

There is no evidence, however, from our research or others', to suggest that informational books about physical science should be reserved for later grades, when children have developed more knowledge about the topics. Rather, indications are that it is necessary to include more age-appropriate informational books about physical and earth and space science in the early grades than is usual currently. Experience with these books will likely help children develop important knowledge and vocabulary that will both improve their comprehension of other books on the subjects and make learning physical science easier for children in later grades.

### Young Boys and Girls Comprehend Informational Texts Equally Well

Do boys comprehend more from informational texts compared with girls? This is an important question because, as we address in the next chapter, research with older children indicates that boys prefer reading informational books more than girls do. Given that people's skills and abilities in a subject are strengthened from their experiences with it, if boys enjoy and read informational books more they may come to comprehend this genre better than girls do. Alternately, perhaps because of gender typing around book topics, which often affects children's choices and interest in what they read (Merisuo-Storm, 2006), girls may understand informational books about "girls' topics" (e.g., animals, babies) better than boys do, and boys may do better than girls with expository books on "boys' topics" (e.g., machines, electricity). These suggestions about possible differences between the sexes are related to boys and girls having different experiences over time with informational books, though, and are therefore not necessarily present with younger children. This is important to know and consider. If young girls and boys are equally able to comprehend informational text, *its use in the earliest grades may prevent the typical differences in reading between the sexes from occurring.*

There is no evidence that, in the early years of school, boys are better able to comprehend informational text than girls are. In our work, we have found that girls and boys were equally able to retell each of the four different informational texts shown in Figure 2.1. Also, boys and girls were comparable on reading comprehension across the four excerpts. In other words, we did not find that girls had an advantage when the text was about stereotypically "girls' topics," such as baby animals (reflected in the *Dolphins* text), or stereotypically "boys' topics," such as machines (reflected in *Levers*).

It may be that in the current climate of fiction-rich early education environments, young girls, who tend to be competent readers, get better at reading fictional genres and therefore improve their reading skills and establish strong reading identities as readers of narrative. However, perhaps this comes at the expense of opportunities for girls to build the skills required for reading and understanding other genres, such as informational text. As we noted in the previous chapter, the set of skills needed for understanding fiction is different from that needed for comprehending other genres. Therefore, strong readers of fiction will not necessarily also become competent consumers of different genres, including science text (Ford et al., 2006). In the later grades, when the use of scientific text is routine, the balance may well swing the other way to favor boys' understanding and learning from these texts.

### Young Children Distinguish Between Narrative Fiction and Informational Text

Children not only comprehend the *content* of informational text, but also, when they routinely experience both narrative and informational books, they develop an understanding that the two genres *have different structures* and *serve different purposes.* This is clearly conveyed by Chad, an average kindergartener. During an individual conversation with one of us, Chad talked about the books he reads at school, including the differences between the informational science books his teacher reads in class and the fiction books that were available in the school's library:

**Adult:**    *What's the difference between the science books that you told me about and books like the one that tells about the ghost stories* [that are in the library]?

**Chad:**    *Well, it's kinda easy. The science books tell things about science and the library books from the library tell, just tell stories. The science books tell things that the library books don't tell. The science books . . . teach kids or adults to be smart, and what's gonna happen and how they* [i.e., animals] *protect themselves and how they eat, how they drink.*

**Adult:**    *And the library books?*

**Chad:**    *They don't make kids smart. They just tell stories . . .*

**Adult:**    *Are these fun?*

**Chad:**    *Yeah, but the science books don't tell the same thing as the library books. They tell how things eat, how they drink.*

Clearly Chad was not confused by sometimes reading books that presented information and sometimes books that told a story. He could distinguish between the genres and appreciate that each type of book had a different purposes. Chad's teacher had not explicitly compared these two genres and noted the functions of each; Chad simply learned from his experiences. However, you may wish to make the differences in genres explicit to your students, as outlined in the Common Core State Standards. For example, you could read both narrative and informational books on the same topic and engage children in discussing what they learned from each, as well as the differences between them. We address strategies for incorporating discussion about informational books into your classroom in Chapter 5.

## IN SUMMARY

Not all of children's early discourse experiences parallel the way that events are commonly structured and sequenced in narrative texts. Children's conversations with more knowledgeable others can be structured around narrative or informational formats, perhaps depending on the type of event and the information of interest. However, there is extremely little known about how parents respond to their children's information-seeking questions—do parents tell stories or give information more often? Regardless, there is clear evidence that children have the capacity to engage in and become familiar with both narrative and expository discourse styles (see also Chapter 7). This dual familiarity calls into question the arguments often made that young children find informational structures (whether spoken or written) uninviting and difficult to comprehend, and that they need to practice with narrative text first, before they can, gradually and with significant training, move on to informational texts. *There is simply no evidence to support these claims!*

## CHAPTER 2 APPLICATIONS FOR PRACTICE

### Try-It-On Activities

The following suggested activities require that you try ideas presented in this chapter in your classroom.

1. Discussion with students about narrative and informational text. Ask your students about their views of different books. Who is speaking? What are they saying that supports points made in this chapter or raises new questions?

2. Taking stock of the classroom library. Consider your classroom library. What proportion of books are narrative texts? What proportion are informational texts?

3. Checking out the school library. Discuss this topic with the school librarian or resource center director. How are volumes chosen? What is observed in student choices? What types of texts are emphasized in library instruction?

4. An informational book a day. Make a plan to read an informational text a day and note the questions and reactions of your students. What did you learn?

## FOR DISCUSSION AND REFLECTION

1. How would the primary grades be different if the majority of teachers *preferred* informational texts more than narrative? Consider the curriculum, choices for student activities and materials, classroom routines, and so on.

2. What instructional decisions need to be made when a narrative book presents information (e.g., *The Very Hungry Caterpillar*)? What are potential opportunities and challenges when books combine narrative with informational text?

3. Describe your reaction to factual questions that your students ask but that you do not have the answers to. How do you typically respond? What is the best way to respond? How comfortable do you feel when young children seek information that you do know or understand?

## HIGHLY RECOMMENDED READING

Zygouris-Coe, V., Wiggins, M. B., & Smith, L. H. (2004). Engaging students with text: The 3–2–1 strategy. *The Reading Teacher, 58,* 381–384.

# 3

# Are Young Children Really Interested in Informational Books?

**A** commonly held concern is that young children don't find informational books interesting and would rather read fictitious stories (Y. Lee et al., 2011). This is not the case, however. Not only can young children understand informational texts—as we discussed in the previous chapter—but young children enjoy reading them. In fact, *young children find informational books just as interesting and motivating as fictional stories* (Caswell & Duke, 1998; Pappas, 1991, 1993). So where does this erroneous view that children find informational books uninteresting come from?

**PAUSE TO REFLECT**

1. Do you read informational books to children with the same amount of enthusiasm and expression that you read story-books?

2. Are there other ways that children might get a message that fictional books are more enjoyable than informational books?

3. Do you think boys prefer informational texts more than girls do? What explains these differences (or lack of differences)?

## EARLY LEARNING EXPERIENCES SHAPE CHILDREN'S MOTIVATION

The early experiences that children have with various school subjects influence the beliefs they develop about those subject areas and about themselves as learners of those subjects (Wigfield & Eccles, 2002). These beliefs, which influence motivation in important ways, include whether children view a subject as

- being *hard or easy* for them,
- *important* for them to learn or not,
- *appropriate* for them to be learning (e.g., "it's not what girls do," "it's not for children my age"),
- *interesting or boring,* and
- something they are or can *be good at.*

Children develop their liking for particular subjects, and their perceptions of being good at those subjects, when they have ongoing, meaningful opportunities to engage in them. For example, positive early experiences with mathematics lead to children enjoying math and believing they are competent at it (Helmke & van Aken, 1995). Conversely, without experiencing a subject or activity, it is very difficult for children to develop positive beliefs about that subject.

## Children's Limited Experience
## Reading Informational Books Restricts
## Their Opportunities to Develop Their Interests

There is very little research about young children's interest in reading different types of genres. However, children's reading motivation in the upper elementary grades and later varies, depending on the type of genre involved (Guthrie et al., 2007). This is likely because children are more familiar with some genres than others. There are significant consequences for these differences, in terms of both motivation for reading different types of books or texts, and motivation for learning content areas beyond reading/language arts.

### *Consequences of Children's Book-Reading*
### *Experiences for Their Reading Motivation*

Children's experiences while they are learning to read influence their enjoyment of reading, as well as their views of themselves as competent readers (Aunola, Leskinen, Onatsu-Arvilommi, & Nurmi, 2002; Chapman, Tunmer, & Pronchow, 2000). This enjoyment and perceived competence is specific to the type of genre involved, so children who encounter only fiction will likely be interested and confident in reading only fiction. Therefore, having limited experience with informational text in the early years restricts the opportunities that children have to develop

- skills that are specific to reading this genre,
- appreciation and enjoyment of this type of book, and
- a view of themselves as being good at reading informational text.

In the United States, where children in the early school grades read and are read fiction almost exclusively, upper elementary and middle-grade students prefer reading fictional narratives to nonfiction books (Harkrader & Moore, 1997). However, *children's preference for fiction is not inevitable* but instead reflects that they have had considerably more experience with fictional stories than with informational books. Children tend to say they prefer fiction because that is what they have experienced, not because they couldn't be equally (or more) interested in nonfiction if it were also familiar and available to them.

Asking children if they are interested in informational books, either about specific topics or in general, is not a reliable way to gauge their interest—children don't have enough experience to really know. This is how researchers have tended to study children's reading motivation, however, and by doing so they have likely influenced the results of their studies. Researchers typically ask children either (1) how much they enjoy reading particular types of books in general, such as science fiction or fairy tales (e.g., Fleener, Morrison, Linek, & Rasinski, 1997), or (2) how much they would like to read books representing different topics and genres, based only on fictitious titles and descriptions (e.g., Harkrader & Moore, 1997). If children are not used to reading informational books, they would be unlikely to say they like this genre, even if it turns out they really would. Children also choose books according to features such as the appeal of the cover and the illustrations (Fleener et al., 1997), which could attract children's interest even if the title does not. Therefore, asking children only about fictitious titles and general categories of books does not give an opportunity for the cover to grab a child's interest. The point we want to make here is that it is preferable to assume that young children *will* enjoy informational books and provide many opportunities for them to do so.

Because of having little experience with nonfiction books, when children are finally faced with reading informational texts, usually around fourth grade, they find understanding this genre more difficult compared with text that has a familiar narrative structure. Because it's not usual to enjoy activities that we find more difficult, it's not surprising that children in these grades would rather read the more familiar and comprehendible (for them) narrative texts. As we have already discussed, the new Common Core State Standards were designed to address this problem by ensuring that children read equal proportions of fictional and informational texts.

*Children Do Enjoy Informational
Books When They Read Them Often*

There is every indication that increasing the amount and quality of experiences that children have with informational books, to a level equivalent to their experiences with narratives, will result in children enjoying the two genres similarly. For example, a successful program was developed by researchers in Maryland to integrate science instruction with teaching reading strategies for both narrative and informational books (Guthrie et al., 2007). After fourth graders received daily instruction for 12 weeks, their interest in reading informational books was linked to increased motivation (compared with that at the start of the program) for all kinds of reading. It was striking that children's interest in reading narrative books was not associated with increased overall reading motivation. This shows that it was the informational text that made the difference in their motivation. Children who were initially not very motivated to read became more motivated once they developed an interest in informational text. However, children's interest in reading narrative text was already influencing their overall reading motivation, presumably because they were familiar with it and this genre constituted most, if not all, of what they read.

Other researchers have also shown that informational, content-specific books are as interesting and motivating to young children as are fictional narratives (Donovan, Smolkin, & Lomax, 2000; Mohr, 2006; Pappas, 1991, 1993). We have found the same with kindergarteners.

*Consequences on Children's
Motivation for Other Content Areas*

Having limited experience with informational books in the early grades has implications for children's learning of content areas beyond reading and language arts, such as science and social studies, because these subjects are often addressed in expository books. Young children typically spend very little time in the classroom learning science and social studies; this may change, however, as a result of the implementation of the Common Core State Standards. Time for science and social studies is necessarily restricted currently by the intense focus on children learning to read, reading narrative books, and, to a lesser extent, learning early mathematics skills. Again, having little time for learning these content areas results in children tending to view the subjects as more difficult than those they have focused on (i.e., science is harder than reading or mathematics). This is the case for science, at least. There has been little, if any, research on young children's views of social studies, perhaps because this subject is featured so little in the early grade curriculum; just 12% of the informational books read by prekindergarten through third-grade teachers address social studies (Yopp & Yopp, 2012).

Children begin school with a natural interest in science-related questions, such as where the sun goes at night or what causes different weather phenomena (Brown, 1997). That interest decreases, however, between upper elementary and high school (Greenfield, 1997). By the upper elementary and middle grades, children also tend to view science as more difficult, less important, and less enjoyable to learn than other school subjects (Andre, Whigham, Hendrickson, & Chambers, 1999; D. R. Baker, 1998). Beliefs about the difficulty, importance, and interest of subject areas are not unimportant—they are major contributors to students' later choices, including their high school classes, postsecondary programs of study, and careers (Wigfield & Eccles, 2002).

*An Illustration of Young Children's
Interest in Informational Books*

We return now to our work with kindergarteners that we introduced in the previous chapter. Recall, we read excerpts (four of which are shown in Figure 2.1) from informational science books to kindergarteners (Mantzicopoulos & Patrick, 2010). Directly after we read each excerpt and the children retold it to us, we asked, *"If I had a longer book like the one we just read, would you like to read it?"* Most children expressed clear interest in the two life science and two physical science texts. Approximately two thirds of the children said they would like to read a longer book similar to the texts *Fins, Wings, and Legs* (about animal movement), *Dolphins,* and *Light.* More than half of them expressed interest in reading another book about simple machines like *What Is a Lever?* The children's responses match what we observed; they were excited and engaged while listening to the informational texts. Across the board, we have found no evidence that young children think informational science books are boring. To the contrary, children usually want to read more of them!

That our young children were equally interested in informational books about physical science as life science fits squarely with what others have found. Although children in the middle grades usually believe that biology is more interesting than other areas of science (Andre et al., 1999; Baram-Tsabari, Sethi, Bry, & Yarden, 2006), *young* children are very interested in questions involving physical science and technology. They ask questions such as *"How does the barcode in the supermarket work?"* (Baram-Tsabari & Yarden, 2005, p. 808) and *"What is the difference between shooting stars and regular stars?"* (Baram-Tsabari et al., 2006, p. 1058). That interest declines, however, during the early grades. For example, children 8 years old and younger are twice as interested in topics in physics than older children are (Baram-Tsabari & Yarden, 2005). It is likely that reading accurate, age-appropriate books in different areas of science early and regularly will help to maintain or increase children's early interest in areas of science such as physics. This is fundamental to children being adequately prepared for high-tech jobs, where there are projected shortages of skilled workers.

In summary, therefore, having little experience with informational text in the early years limits the development of children's appreciation for (1) the structure and format of informational text; (2) discipline-specific vocabulary and the functions and structure of its reading, writing, and discourse; and (3) discipline-specific concepts and content. It also restricts the development of children's abilities related to these three areas, and the relative difficulty that results in later years will likely detract from their enjoyment and interest. Following from these points, it may be that engaging children regularly in reading informational text in the early grades will allow them to enjoy it, both then and in the future. It is also likely that children's natural interest in content areas such as science will be maintained into later grades; then, when they read informational text, children will be able to focus on fascinating situations and answers to intriguing questions rather than getting bogged down in unfamiliar text.

## Boys and Girls Are Equally Interested in Informational Books

Although all evidence points to young children's strong interest in informational books, girls and boys generally have different reading preferences. In general, girls tend to be more interested than boys in reading. With this in mind, when girls and boys are asked about the types of books they prefer to read, boys tend to say they enjoy reading nonfiction more than fiction, and considerably more than girls do. In contrast, girls prefer fiction (Harkrader & Moore, 1997; Merisuo-Storm, 2006; Yopp & Yopp, 2006). For example, all third-grade girls in one study named fiction when asked by the researchers about the kinds of books they like to read (Ford et al., 2006).

When asked about particular subjects they like to read within the nonfiction category, boys and girls also report different preferences from each other. The most popular nonfiction books for boys are about sports, with books about space, earth science, and "how-to" science books clustering in a distant second place. Girls, conversely, say they like informational books about art and hobbies most, but science topics—the human body and "how-to" science books—are ranked next (Harkrader & Moore, 1997). We turn now to consider similarities and differences between boys' and girls' interests in reading about various science topics.

## Boys' and Girls' Interests in Science Topics

There have been more than 30 years of research into science-related differences between males and females, driven in part by concern that disproportionately fewer girls and women choose advanced classes and careers that involve science and technology. One line of work has shown that boys' and girls' choices are a consequence of gender-related differences in the interests they develop. As part of identifying these differences, researchers have asked about the preferences of boys and girls, mostly from fourth grade or beyond, to learn about general areas of science (e.g., biology, physics) or specific science topics or questions (e.g., optics, why we depend on other plants and animals). These studies include identifying gender differences in the kinds of science books that girls and boys read, how much they like learning particular topics, or how interested they are in learning about those topics in the future, in addition to specific out-of-school science-related interests.

Boys' and girls' interests diverge along stereotypical gender lines. Boys tend to be more interested in physical science compared with both their own interest in life science and girls' interest in physical science (Baram-Tsabari et al., 2006). Boys report greater interest in topics such as electricity, x-rays, light and sound, mechanics, and lasers (Dawson, 2000; A. T. Jones & Kirk, 1990; M. G. Jones, Howe, & Rua, 2000). Their out-of-school activities also involve more physical science, such as playing with batteries, circuit boards, and ropes and pulleys, compared with girls (Greenfield, 1997; M. G. Jones et al., 2000). The life sciences, conversely, are more interesting to girls, compared with physical science and boys' interest in life science. Girls are most interested in biology-related topics, such as animals and their babies, diseases, plants, and nutrition (Dawson, 2000; Ford et al., 2006; M. G. Jones et al., 2000).

There are many areas of science, however, that girls and boys say are equally interesting to them. For example, when given a long list of popular topics, both boys and girls gave top ratings to topics such as earthquakes, crystals, heating and burning, water purity, poisonous animals, and how to use science instruments (Dawson, 2000). Studies have also been inconsistent in terms of interest in other topics, such as astrophysics or space science (e.g., rockets, space missions, the solar system) and earth science (e.g., volcanoes). Some studies report that boys are more interested in space science than girls are (Dawson, 2000; M. G. Jones et al., 2000) but other studies find that boys' and girls' interests are comparable (Baram-Tsabari & Yarden, 2005). Similarly, there is no consistent sex difference in interest for earth science topics, which are either more interesting to boys (Dawson, 2000), more interesting to girls (M. G. Jones et al., 2000), or equally interesting to both sexes (Baram-Tsabari & Yarden, 2005).

We believe it is useful to look beyond the surface of apparent differences in interest for science topics, to consider underlying concepts that are common to both boys' and girls' typical preferences. For example, although girls express greater interest than boys in learning about rainbows, what they are, and why you can see them, boys say they are more interested than girls in light and optics (M. G. Jones et al., 2000); these topics can surely be presented so that they appeal highly to both sexes. Similarly, girls' preferences for learning about diseases and medical technology may be addressed along with boys' interests in technological devices and lasers (A. T. Jones & Kirk, 1990; M. G. Jones et al., 2000). Also, the way that different topics are framed and presented to children can make tremendous differences to the enthusiasm they bring to learning about them. For example, in one study, 88% of fourth-grade girls said they like reading nonfiction books about animals; however, only about half that number (46%) said they were interested in science books (Harkrader & Moore, 1997). Clearly, these young girls did not consider factual information about animals to be part of science.

Different opportunities in the early school years for girls and boys to read a variety of informational and narrative books may be responsible for the gender-specific preferences for fiction and information texts that we typically see in later childhood. This is unclear at present, because topics for reading that are of most interest to young boys and girls have not yet been identified. However, we have asked kindergarteners whether or not they would like to read books similar to the excerpts shown in Chapter 2.

The young boys and girls we worked with expressed comparable levels of interest in reading the different expository texts, regardless of whether the text was about the stereotypically "girls' topic" of animal babies or stereotypically "boys' topic" of machines (Mantzicopoulos & Patrick, 2010). Therefore, even though young boys' and girls' relative preferences of genre and topics may differ (e.g., Dawson, 2000; Harkrader & Moore, 1997; M. G. Jones et al., 2000), informational science books about a variety of topics can be highly appealing to both sexes.

## Using Informational Books in Content Areas Can Capitalize on Children's Interests

The predominance of fiction over informational, content-specific genres in the early school years may compromise not only young children's learning and comprehension but also their long-term interest and engagement. Boys, it is argued, would likely read much better if school reading involved the kinds of books that appealed to them (Worthy, Moorman, & Turner, 1999; Young & Brozo, 2001). Informational books include many topics that boys tend to be interested in. Using such books within content-area and language arts instruction is likely to promote boys' interest in both subject areas. The same applies to young girls, who, as we have discussed here, have interests in many science-related topics but few opportunities to learn about them by reading informational texts.

Because the development of reading skills is genre-specific (Palincsar & Duke, 2004), it is crucial that boys and girls develop views of themselves as skilled readers who enjoy reading for a variety of purposes and across different content areas. For this to happen, children must be provided with rich experiences with a variety of both narrative and informational genres.

## CHAPTER 3 APPLICATIONS FOR PRACTICE

### Try-It-On Activities

The following suggested activities require that you try ideas presented in this chapter in your classroom.

1. Are young children really interested in informational books? Consider your beliefs, those of your colleagues, parents, and students by gathering answers to this question and then reflect upon how your findings support or do not support this chapter.

2. Record yourself reading a narrative and an informational text. What do you notice? How does this self-study inform your practice? What needs to happen next?

## FOR DISCUSSION AND REFLECTION

1. How do teachers break the cycle of limited experience with informational books other than by just adding more informational texts?

2. Discuss the major pedagogical issues around gender and informational text. For example: What might be the relationship between young boys' lower levels of success in school and in reading different genres? How does the predominance of female primary teachers shape the curriculum and boys' achievement, motivation, and interest? Is your classroom "girl-friendly"?

## HIGHLY RECOMMENDED READING

Correia, M. P. (2011, November). Fiction vs. informational texts: Which will kindergartners choose? *Young Children*, 100–104. Retrieved from http://www.naeyc.org/files/yc/file/201111/Correia_Fiction_vs_Informational_Texts_Online%201111.pdf

Duke, N. K. (2003). *Information books in early childhood.* Washington, DC: National Association for the Education of Young Children. Retrieved from http://journal.naeyc.org/btj/200303/InformationBooks.pdf

# 4

# What Should I Consider When Selecting Informational Books?

During the last decade, there has been considerable interest in using informational picture books as a way to strengthen language arts and also to include content areas such as social studies and science into the curriculum (Roser & Keehn, 2002; Saul, 2004). This approach is now formalized in the Common Core State Standards (National Governors Association Center for Best Practices & Council of Chief State School Officers, 2010) and adopted by 45 of the 50 states, some of which have begun implementing these standards. Ensuring that young children have opportunities to engage with informational books balances instruction so that it is not always tipped in favor of narrative genres.

From an *English language arts point of view,* using informational texts

- broadens children's literacy experiences,
- builds sophisticated and specialized vocabulary, and
- increases their familiarity with a range of different text conventions (Hall, Sabey, & McLellan, 2005).

From a *content-area perspective,* using informational texts

- supports student inquiry,
- contributes to discussions on discipline-specific topics, and
- allows children to learn about phenomena and events that they cannot experience firsthand (Ford, 2004).

Not all informational books are equally beneficial for young children—some lead to higher quality learning than others. Therefore, it is crucial to consider the quality and appropriateness of each book before you use it in your classroom. Given the already large and ever-growing number of informational children's books available on a variety of topics, how should you select books for your classroom? What criteria should guide your decisions so that the informational books benefit your students most?

We illustrate the way that a book's genre and quality of the content can influence what children learn by discussing a study that involved children reading *Dear Mr. Blueberry,* a book about whales (Mayer, 1995). Specifically, Mayer (1995) set out to investigate whether children learn and remember science facts better when they are embedded in a story form. For this purpose, she selected *Dear Mr. Blueberry* (James, 1991), a book that communicates facts about whales within the presumably facilitative context of realistic-but-fictional narrative. The focus of the book revolves around a young girl, Emily, who corresponds with Mr. Blueberry to ask for information about whales. Each of Emily's letters reveals misconceptions or inaccuracies that she has about whales, such as they live in ponds and they smile, and these misconceptions are carefully addressed by Mr. Blueberry. His responses provide information about the features, habits, and habitats of whales.

Mayer's (1995) results, based on individual readings of the book to 16 children (two boys and two girls at each grade level from kindergarten to third grade) showed that *using a mixed genre* (i.e., information + realistic narrative) *for teaching content-specific concepts is not most effective.* In particular, when the children retold the story and answered questions about whales (e.g., their size, eating habits, habitat, parts of the story that "are not true"), it was evident that they had learned a mixture of a few accurate and many inaccurate, or "pseudo," facts. The latter were part of Emily's original misconceptions (e.g., whales "have names, can jump from ponds to oceans [and] eat fish and shrimp") that, despite being corrected by Mr. Blueberry, infiltrated children's thinking about whales. Therefore, the study generated doubts about the benefits of *genre hybridization*—the blending of stories with facts—when using books to teach science content, and drew attention to the need for criteria to guide the selection and use of informational books in the classroom.

Mayer (1995) argued that educators need to approach informational books from a stance that considers the functions of these texts in relation to criteria that have implications for both language arts and content-area learning. These include the type of book, ease of distinguishing fact from fiction, the accuracy and misrepresentation of facts in the text, portrayal of characters (including animals), and gender equity. Similar criteria have been outlined by the National Science Teachers Association (NSTA, 2011) and are used each year to select texts for the *Outstanding Science Trade Books for Students K–12.* Additional criteria to consider are the content-specific subgenres and their potential uses for instruction (Ford, 2004).

We have synthesized the evidence for choosing informational books into guidelines across three broad dimensions: book genres, quality of content, and quality of illustrations (see Figure 4.1). Our recommendations come from both the developmental and the educational literature about young children's competencies during read-alouds with diverse texts. Because there is extremely little evidence on using

**Figure 4.1**  Criteria for Evaluating Informational Books for Young Children

| Book Genre | Quality of Content | Quality of Illustrations |
|---|---|---|
| Fictional-Hybrid-Informational | Clear Concepts, Up-to-Date Knowledge | Iconicity |
| Content Subgenres | Oversimplifications | Attention to Equity |
| Considerations:<br>• Ease of Distinguishing Fact From Fiction<br>• Ease of Distinguishing Accurate From Realistic Content | Accurate Portrayal of Time | |

informational social studies books with young readers, we use examples that primarily involve science texts.

## BOOK GENRES

### The Continuum of Fictional-Hybrid-Informational Books

In Chapter 1, our discussion of fictional and expository (purely informational) texts addressed them as two distinct genres at opposing ends of a continuum. In between these two ends are hybrid genres (e.g., *Dear Mr. Blueberry*), characterized by texts that are based on combinations of factual and realistic or fictional content. We represent this continuum—from fiction to information—in Figure 4.2 using examples of children's books about dinosaurs. Recall that at one end of the continuum are fictional storybooks (e.g., *Eddie*

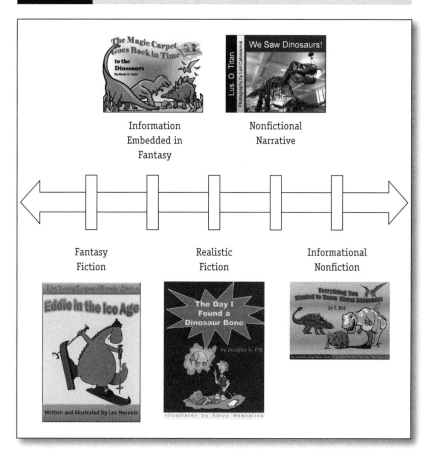

Figure 4.2    Fiction–Information Continuum

*in the Ice Age*), which include fantastical, fanciful elements (e.g., a dinosaur learning to ski) and are intended to provide exciting and entertaining content for the reader. At the opposite end (e.g., *Everything You Wanted to Learn About Dinosaurs*), informational books are written to provide factual, up-to-date knowledge about a topic (e.g., dinosaur types, characteristics, habits) and conform to the characteristics of informational texts presented in Chapter 1. Of course, not all texts at the end of the information continuum include broad, comprehensive topic coverage like *Everything You Wanted to Learn About Dinosaurs* does.

In between the two extremes, hybrid, dual-purpose books combine structures of both stories and informational books and have facts woven into the story (Donovan & Smolkin, 2001). Some dual-purpose books include a mixture of fact and fantasy. For example, *The Magic Carpet Goes Back in Time to the Dinosaurs* tells the story of a group of children who are inadvertently whisked into the air and transported back in time to learn about dinosaurs. It is similar to books in the popular *Magic School Bus* series, which place a number of science facts within the context of a fantastical story plot. With each new topical theme, the Magic School Bus serves as the vehicle that transports children to places where they experience the content to be learned directly, such as inside the human body, out in space to learn about planets and the solar system, or to the past to encounter dinosaurs.

Unlike the *Magic School Bus* texts that blend fantasy with science facts, other dual-purpose books (e.g., *We Saw Dinosaurs!*) are based on realistic narrative plots (e.g., a child visits the museum with his family to learn about dinosaurs) that provide factual information about a topic as the story unfolds. In this case, the science facts are still embedded in a storied, plausible format that is easy for children to follow and identify with.

Hybrid, dual-purpose texts for content-area instruction enjoy considerable popularity, fueled by arguments that stories are instrumental for young children's comprehension. Many such texts are included in the National Science Teachers Association (2011) *Outstanding Science Trade Books for Students K–12* and the *Notable Social Studies Trade Books for Young People* published each year by the National Council for the Social Studies (NCSS, 2012a). Therefore, being familiar with the structures and purposes of "pure" and hybrid texts is an important step to evaluating the appropriateness of different books for instruction and the implications of using them for children's learning. It is crucial to consider (1) what aspects of the disciplinary content are represented and how (i.e., the content subgenre), (2) whether or not the combination of fact and fiction interferes with children's learning, and (3) quality issues related to accuracy. We address these topics next.

## Book Content Subgenres and Uses

Within language arts it is important for children to be familiar with a range of text genres along the fictional-informational continuum just described; experiencing this variety helps orient readers to important genre-specific structural features of books. However, because informational texts are featured as appropriate and effective content-area resources, it is equally important to consider the fit of texts with content-specific subgenres, or the ways in which a discipline (e.g., life or physical science) is portrayed in different texts (Ford, 2004). For instance, whether the content is represented as a collection of facts, as the outcome of inquiry-related processes, or as part of an interesting story has implications for how a text may be used in instruction.

We illustrate the way that a book's use is influenced by its subgenre by presenting, in Figure 4.3, a useful outline developed by Ford (2004, pp. 152–153) to address science-related subgenres typically found in informational texts. Content subgenres (e.g., facts, experiments, biography, geography) are listed in the left column, and examples for how these texts may be used in instruction are shown in the far right column. Although Ford has related the subgenres to science content, most are applicable also to other content areas. Even the subgenre of "experiments," which may be thought to exemplify science inquiry, does apply to some but not all areas of social studies (e.g., history, geography). Nevertheless, books that rely on methods of inquiry (even if they are not experiments) in history or geography, though probably few, reflect this subgenre.

Note that Ford included "story" as a subgenre in her scheme, something that once again highlights the rather prominent place of this type of text in the curriculum. Considering that in storied texts real-world facts are interlaced with fiction, it's important to examine the extent to and the circumstances under which young children are able to discern reality from fantasy, particularly when they have few or no firsthand experiences with the topics covered in a text.

**Figure 4.3**    Text Subgenres and Uses

| Science-focused subgenre | ◄──────────────────────► | Use |
|---|---|---|
| Facts | The primary purpose of this type of book is to provide factual information about a topic or series of topics. The books often contain expository text, often descriptive or taxonomic. They may also provide scientific explanations.<br>Popular formats: single topic of interests to children (e.g., volcanoes, Saturn, baby animals), question and answer, field guide | Resources/references during investigations<br>Generate questions or ideas<br>Confirm/disconfirm science claims<br>Identify/classify unknowns |
| Experiments | This book focus presents collections of projects or experiments that illustrate scientific concepts.<br>Popular formats: science fair ideas, experiments, activities, projects | Ideas for classroom activities<br>Methods, procedures for investigations<br>Standards for collecting data |
| Biography/history | These books explain the history of a scientific field, or tell the story of a scientist past or present. They tell students something about the way science is done or the people who do science.<br>Popular formats: biographies of scientists, profiles of science careers, historical science events (space program, the Enlightenment) | Introduce students to scientific community, scientists<br>History of controversial science topics |
| Geography/travel | These books present nature, habitats, ecosystems from a variety of locations around the world. They often combine biology, anthropology, and nature.<br>Popular formats: rainforest expeditions, habitat/biome books, conservation books | Integration with social studies |
| Artistic expression | These books use art, poetry, song to express the beauty of the natural world.<br>Popular formats: picture books, art books, poetry | Engage learners in content area<br>Integration with literacy, art |
| Story | These books use fictional narratives to tell stories related to science or with science themes.<br>Popular formats: science fiction, fiction, fables and legends with nature themes | Engage learners in content area<br>Integration with literacy |

*Source*: Ford (2004, pp. 152–153).

## Ease of Distinguishing Fact From Fiction

As we discussed in Chapter 2, young children *do* develop understandings that different texts accomplish different goals: fiction is for fun whereas exposition is for learning things. By the time they are 5 years old, children use cues from the context to infer whether novel, unfamiliar events exist in the real world (Woolley & Van Reet, 2006). Moreover, they are able to differentiate *factuality* (i.e., whether events and characters in a book did or did not exist at some point in time) from *possibility* (i.e., whether characters and events can happen in real life). Regardless of story content (i.e., realistic or fantastical), children are likely to understand that the characters were developed for the purposes of the book and do not exist in real life (Woolley & Cox, 2007). In other words, the characters are "pretend" or "just in the book" (Woolley & Cox, 2007, p. 685). However, when asked about the possibility that characters and events portrayed in fantastical and realistic stories can or could exist in real life, children were more likely to respond in favor of the realistic scenarios. That is, even if they recognized that characters and events were created by the author, children were more likely to claim that an event could potentially occur in real life if it were described in the context of a realistic (as opposed to a fantastical) story.

In related research that examined children's ability to infer the reality status of historical characters, it was shown that older (5–7-year-old) children tend to be quite accurate in their judgments. Specifically, children use contextual cues to determine whether the story events can happen and then judge the reality of characters within that context (Corriveau, Kim, Schwalen, & Harris, 2009). Characters and events depicted in realistic historical contexts are judged to have existed at one point in time.

Together, this evidence suggests that texts with realistic content may be better suited for facilitating connections between the textual events and children's lives. Also, it implies that even young children (4-year-olds and 5-year-olds) have the capacity to judge the reality/fictional status of entities and phenomena presented in realistic genres. Conversely, indications are that fictional narrative based on fantastical scenarios with few added traces of factual, content-specific information may have a very limited role in content-area instruction.

## Ease of Distinguishing Accurate From Realistic Content in Dual-Purpose Texts

At this point, although realistic genres may seem to emerge as the preferred medium for content-area instruction, it's important not to lose sight of the fact that realistic narrative is not necessarily error free or factual. Realistic narrative may be confusing when it includes inaccuracies that children consider highly plausible and therefore believable, given their knowledge and experiences. For instance, the belief (noted in one of Emily's letters in *Dear Mr. Blueberry*) that whales live in ponds falls well within the bounds of possibility for young readers who may have had the opportunity to see whales in large ponds during visits to the zoo. Perhaps this explains findings that parallel Mayer's (1995) in other studies that have used either *Dear Mr. Blueberry* (Rice, 2002) or other social studies– and science-related dual-purpose texts (Brabham, Boyd, & Edgington, 2010) to explore children's learning. There seems to be agreement that children are likely to absorb both accurate and realistic-but-inaccurate facts when inaccuracies are plausible within the realm of children's familiar experiences.

This brings up the question of the teacher's role in ensuring that the unique features and information that children should attend to in each book are made explicit. However, research has not systematically addressed this issue. In an early study, Jetton (1994) examined the benefits of calling children's attention to the factual elements in *Dear Mr. Blueberry* prior to the reading. In one condition, children were cued to the informational content of the book ("This BOOK . . . is going to tell you a lot of interesting things about the life of whales," p. 114), whereas in a second condition, children were cued to the story content ("This book is a STORY . . . about a little girl, Emily, who loves whales," p. 114). Contrary to expectation, Jetton found that, after listening to the story, both groups of students "responded more to the story events than the information about whales" (p. 127). It appears that providing a general, overall information-related framework prior to sharing a book with children does not minimize their vulnerability to believing the realistic but inaccurate elements in a story.

In all, this body of literature provides useful information about children's capacity to make complex judgments about real and fantastical information contained in printed books, with minimal cuing from others and without discussion of the story. However, it provides few clues about how children come to think about new knowledge (including the ability to distinguish fanciful from factual content) within an instructional context that fosters opportunities for vocabulary building, discussion, argumentation, and evidence related to the reading(s). Arguably, the teacher's role in facilitating children's knowledge construction is critical in this regard. Jetton's (1994) study, based on the idea of cuing children to the purposes of the reading, fell short of exploring the consequences of rich and purposeful instruction. Therefore, depending on the teacher's goals, it may be useful to include a hybrid text or a combination of several fictional and informational texts to create opportunities for children to discuss, evaluate, and reason about the factual and fictional content. In this endeavor, the teacher's attention to issues of content accuracy, discussed next, is paramount to the construction of knowledge that is not premised on elaborations of inaccurate, "pseudo" facts.

## QUALITY AND ACCURACY OF CONTENT

When they read stories that combine factual and fictional content, young children may not have either the background knowledge or the cognitive resources to evaluate the accuracy and potential utility of new and seemingly factual information provided in a text. Moreover, in the process of learning content-specific information (e.g., *"Boys and girls, in the book* A Very Hungry Caterpillar, *the author tells us about how a caterpillar grows . . ."*), children may actually perceive books that are introduced by their teachers as accurate when in fact they may not be. Children and college students alike hold beliefs that information must be correct because they heard it from their teacher (e.g., in science class; Rice, 2002). In line with this, young children are likely to believe and use information shared by adults who are viewed as sources of expertise (Corriveau & Harris, 2009). Books may be seen as one source of expertise, particularly when they are shared by familiar and knowledgeable others such as teachers or parents. Therefore, evaluating a book's content for clarity, completeness, and accuracy of information before using it in your classroom may suggest different ways to introduce the book and discuss its content with your students. Several components related to accuracy include the following: (1) recognizable topic knowledge, (2) oversimplifications, and (3) attention to the passage of time.

## Recognizable, Up-to-Date Topic Knowledge

Clearly recognizable topic knowledge (theories, facts, concepts) that is up to date and appropriately and logically sequenced for the reader is an important characteristic of effective texts (NSTA, 2011). Unfortunately, even books that claim to be purely informational may have gaps or outdated information. Recent studies show that informational science books contain approximately one inaccuracy per book (Norris et al., 2008). However, books about physical science topics have twice as many errors as texts on life science. A recent examination of 109 elementary-level picture books about plant reproduction showed that 69 of them (almost two thirds!) contained errors (Schussler, 2008). These errors included not explaining how plant reproduction occurs, not being specific enough (e.g., not making it clear that the fruit develops in the place where the flower is located), and using terminology incorrectly.

Some children's books about plant growth claim that plants take their food from the soil. This is a common misconception that may be further reinforced when children, on being called to connect their own experiences to the text, describe "feeding" their plants at home by placing plant food in the soil. Unless you address it directly, the statement in the book encourages the belief that plant roots are like animals' mouths that consume sources of energy for the organism. This misrepresentation of knowledge obscures the fact that, unlike other organisms, plants use energy from the sun to absorb nutrients, water, and carbon dioxide to *produce* food.

Undeniably, young children's background knowledge and cognitive skills are important considerations when teaching disciplinary content. Young children do not have the background knowledge and/or the sophisticated thinking that is necessary to understand many biological and physical phenomena. However, young children's inability to come to a fully fledged, scientifically accurate understanding of various phenomena and processes should not serve as the reason to deliberately exclude certain topics from discussion, particularly when children are interested in and ask about them. In the case of photosynthesis, a simple explanation—brief and unelaborated—that plants make their own food using the sun, presented in the book or introduced by the teacher, is an appropriate option. Consider the similarity of this scenario with one shared by Gelman (2009) about a young student who, in a lesson on plant reproduction, learned from her teacher that there are both male and female plants. Although young children may not be able to understand the gender of plants immediately and comprehensively, they can nevertheless begin laying down a conceptual foundation (e.g., "plants come in different types and this is somehow relevant to reproduction") that can be built on over time. Therefore, a short, uncomplicated statement can serve as a placeholder for later learning (Gelman, 2009). Similarly, in the previous photosynthesis example, the statement that plants make their own food may also serve as a placeholder and lay the groundwork for the continuing growth of more complex understandings.

An important omission in informational texts in the area of science is the lack of attention to the scientific process (Ford, 2006; Schroeder, Mckeough, Graham, Stock, & Bizanz, 2009). Although books frequently mention methods of collecting evidence (e.g., observation, asking questions, using tools, experimenting), there is extremely little information about how disciplinary knowledge is developed by thinking and reasoning from that evidence. In particular, science trade books that are appropriate for the early grades (i.e., K–3) tend to portray science as a collection of facts. Even if the information is up to date and accurate, facts alone are not sufficient for students to develop an understanding of the nature and practice of science and its role in society (Schroeder et al., 2009). The commonplace "science is merely a collection of facts" approach is inconsistent with current reform agendas that emphasize learners developing scientific literacy through an awareness of the processes of science (e.g., inquiry, reflection) and how what we understand scientifically is influenced by social and cultural thinking (National Research Council, 2012). Because of misconceptions that young children are not able to engage in and reason about science, there is a lack of informational books that go beyond presenting science as a collection of facts (Schroeder et al., 2009). Teachers, therefore, need to consciously fill this gap and address the *nature* of science in their instructional program. For example, this may include discussions of how people can go about finding out answers to their questions or actually conducting inquiry activities so that children gain experience with processes such as predicting, observing, gathering data, recording, and drawing conclusions.

## Oversimplifications

A frequent error in informational books that is likely to invite misconceptions involves omitting information by oversimplifying the science concepts they address (Norris et al., 2008). Consider the statement "Plants need food," accompanied by a picture of a plant with its roots shown underground, as in Figure 4.4). This is not incorrect. However, the picture and the

**Figure 4.4**    An Example of Oversimplification

**Plants need food.**

*Source:* Photo from iStockphoto.

accompanying text may encourage the common misconception that we just noted in the previous section—that plants take in their food from the soil. Although paring down information to the point of oversimplification, in and of itself, does not make a book less useful (assuming that the remaining book content is appropriate), it signals that the text needs to be supplemented with discussion about the concept—in this case, that plants make their own food; we elaborate on this point in the next chapter. As long as you are aware of the potential for misconceptions, you can address what children already know and understand about plant growth, as well as introduce new concepts, such as the idea that plants make their own food.

## Portraying the Passage of Time Accurately

Oversimplification that involves the passing of time also occurs commonly in children's informational books. We have encountered this issue in several science books that address the process of growth and development. To continue on the subject of plant growth, let's consider *Isn't It Strange?* (Polette, 2004), a book about the growth of different living things from an early to a fully grown stage. Several living things are included throughout the book, with each pictured at a couple of points in time—for example, a tadpole and a frog, a seed and a yellow sunflower, a human baby and a child. We show two pages of the book in Figure 4.5, where an acorn is shown on one page (*"an acorn sprouts"*) and full-sized trees on the next (*"and becomes a tree"*). Without explicit discussion, children may have difficulty grasping not only the concept of time needed for this growth, but also the idea that different kinds of living things follow different timetables. For example, it is not clear from this book that it takes much less time for a seed to grow into a sunflower than for an acorn to grow into an oak tree. Again, adding this information while reading and talking about the book will help children develop a clearer understanding.

**Figure 4.5**    Accurate Portrayal of the Passage of Time: An Example

| an acorn sprouts | and becomes a tree |

*Source*: Polette (2004), pp. 8–9.

## Accurate Portrayal of the Passage of Time: An Example

Although the excerpt from *Isn't It Strange?* was shown as an example of how potential misconceptions may develop with regard to the passage of time, we do not wish to suggest that a book such as this doesn't serve a useful purpose for instruction.

Indeed, we have found this book to be an excellent tool in the context of instructional activities designed to access children's prior knowledge about growth and as a way to engage children in thinking about different organisms (e.g., the changes that they undergo to reach adult status and the time it takes for these changes to unfold). As in other cases of oversimplification, you can use the lack of details to create a space for children to generate questions and engage in discussion, and therefore to develop new knowledge that connects the missing pieces or gaps in the text.

## QUALITY OF ILLUSTRATIONS

### Realistic Representation or Iconicity

The quality of illustrations and the compatibility between text and illustrations are crucial for promoting children's learning from informational books (NSTA, 2011). Photographs or high-quality drawings that show organisms in their natural habitats and are appropriately scaled contribute to better learning and comprehension than cartoon figures or caricatures do. Illustrations that are connected with and represent the text well help children construct mental models and make better inferences from the information described in the text (Tare, Chiong, Ganea, & DeLoache, 2010). This perhaps explains why children are better able to apply solutions to problems that they have read about when the story shows real people compared with stories with fantasy characters (Richert & Smith, 2011). Importantly, *iconicity*, or the level of realistic representation in pictures, influences the extent to which children transfer the information from the text to new situations. The more realistic the book's picture, the greater the transfer is (Ganea et al., 2008); this highlights how useful informational texts are for children learning about the world.

### Attention to Equity

Many reports have noted the pervasive stereotype of science as an activity that takes place in laboratories run by unconventional individuals—scientists—who are usually males in white coats and thick glasses (Barman, 1999; Buldu, 2006). Although most kindergarteners say they are not familiar with what science involves, some believe that science is not appropriate for them—that it is meant for people who are older and more knowledgeable than they are (Mantzicopulos, Samarapungavan, & Patrick, 2009). Of note, when we asked kindergarteners if they knew about science, those who said they did had developed stereotypical images of scientists (e.g., male, nerdy, wearing glasses and a lab coat, having crazy hair, using laboratory equipment to do bizarre experiments with chemicals; Finson, 2002). For example, they told us:

**Roger:**  *Science is like when you have potions and stuff and they turn into different things.*

**Pablo:**  *(What do you think you can learn in science?) How to make gross stuff. (What sort of gross stuff?) Like disgusting foods, like Dr. Dreadful!*

**Mario:**  *Science is like people who are frozen, or make little people, or make little monsters.*

**Trevor:**  *In science you make a rabbit (How would you do that?) Bring a potion and do it.*

These children's views of science appeared to come from out-of-school experiences with store-bought science materials (e.g., volcano kits), toys (e.g., Dr. Dreadful Freaky Food Lab), storybooks, or television cartoons. Picture books of all genres provide opportunities for children to form beliefs and attitudes about gender, race, class, and disability. Informational books provide a powerful opportunity to show inclusive and realistic notions of individuals who are involved with specific disciplines. This includes showing men and women of all backgrounds, in a range of locations, and working closely with colleagues and the public, not just alone.

The extent to which diversity is represented in images within children's science-related informational books—in either typical public libraries or the *Outstanding Science Trade Books for Students in K–12* (OSTB)—is disappointing (Ford, 2006; Neutze, 2008). Caucasians are shown in 88% of the images in OSTB collections from 1973–2005 (Neutze, 2008). There are few images of women scientists and even fewer of racially diverse individuals. Portrayals of scientists in informational texts show a prevalence of stereotypical images, with the overwhelming majority of scientists being white males (Ford, 2006). Descriptions of personal characteristics (e.g., curious, excited, careful, skeptical) are present but rare, whereas messages about children, who are sometimes portrayed as scientists, convey the oversimplified message that "anyone who acts like a scientist *is* a scientist" (Ford, 2006, p. 229) and that science involves conformity to step-by-step directions (Ford, 2006).

Absent from the discussion of representation of people who are involved with the practice of science are individuals with disabilities. This omission implicitly reinforces common stereotypes that individuals with special needs are less capable, less engaged, or incapacitated by a single disability (Brenna, 2008), and therefore are unable to do science. On the positive side, images of science settings and methods (e.g., observing, data gathering, recording) are very diverse, a move away from the past tendency to show science stereotypically as a solitary, laboratory activity (Neutze, 2008).

## In Conclusion: Choosing Texts and Their Implications for Classroom Use

In this chapter, we reviewed a number of criteria that touch upon issues of text quality and carry crucial implications for classroom use. In all cases, after you have determined that a book may be suitable for use in your classroom, trying the book out with your students (always keeping a keen eye on their responses and engagement) is a very good way to establish how good the book is. After all, quality is not "strictly . . . an inherent characteristic of a book but . . . something that is defined through interaction with readers" (Teale, 2003, p. 126).

In closing, we highlight two additional points: (1) the need for publically accessible reviews of outstanding texts for children and (2) the fit of the text to your curriculum goals.

## The Need for Accessible Ratings

Many of the criteria outlined in this chapter are used to arrive at selections of high-quality informational texts in science (e.g., OSTB; NSTA, 2011). In social studies, the selection of outstanding books (*Notable Social Studies Trade Books for Young People;* NCSS, 2012a, p. 2) comes from reviews of texts that

> emphasize human relations, represent a diversity of groups and are sensitive to a broad range of cultural experiences, present an original theme or a fresh slant on a traditional topic, are easily readable and of high literary quality, have a pleasing format, and, where appropriate, include illustrations that enrich the text.

The NSTA books are matched to the National Science Content Standards (e.g., Life Science, Physical and Space Science, Science & Technology) whereas the NCSS books are matched to thematic social studies standards (e.g., culture, civic ideals, global connections). This information, along with the appropriateness of each book for specific grade levels, is published with the brief book abstracts and is helpful for teachers who may be looking for books that cover specific topics.

Something that is absent from both the NSTA and the NCSS lists, as well as from publications that use books from these lists to compile lesson plans (e.g., Ansberry & Morgan, 2005), are *actual quality ratings along specific criteria* of genre and content quality. It is unrealistic to think that teachers, beyond developing sensitivity to the implications of text quality for the learners, have extra time to personally review collections of informational books and rate them on indicators of quality. For this reason, and considering that professional associations already have review processes in place, it would be important for teachers to have access to this information.

Collections of lesson plans using informational texts (e.g., *Picture Perfect Science Lessons;* Ansberry & Morgan, 2005) do an excellent job showing ways in which particular books may be used along with inquiry activities to address content-specific standards. However, books are usually presented uncritically in these collections, which may give the impression that there are no potential issues for reading them in the classroom. We illustrate this point with an example from *The Popcorn Book* (dePaola, 1984)—an NSTA-recommended book that includes information such as how and why popcorn pops and how it was heated by Native Americans. In addition to this factual information, the book tells and shows about a particularly hot summer's day when corn popped while still growing in the fields. Readers see corn in the fields popping spontaneously, flying off the corn stalks, as the sun beats down (see Figure 4.6). Once the corn has popped, it looks like a storm has blanketed the fields with snow; a farmer has taken out a snow shovel, and a child has put on a scarf, hat, ear warmers, and mittens.

**Figure 4.6**  Example From *The Popcorn Book*

*Source*: de Paola (1978).

Additional information that cues teachers to each book's shortcomings or potential for students' misinterpretation, given the criteria discussed in this chapter, may help teachers address omissions or oversimplifications that might lead to distortions or reinforce misconceptions and stereotypes.

## Fit of Texts to Curriculum Goals

An important consideration with using books as part of your instruction is their overall fit with your instructional goals. Science educators increasingly call for instructional approaches that integrate science inquiry with literacy activities as an effective and realistic path toward high-quality science instruction (Marx & Harris, 2006; Yore, Bisanz, & Hand, 2003), and the same holds for social studies education (Marinak & Gambrell, 2009). However, let us be clear that we do not advocate that all content-area instruction be included within the *reading* curriculum. We agree with Brophy and Alleman (2009, p. 363), who made the following important points about social studies instruction but which apply equally to science:

1. *Target High Quality.* Well-chosen high-quality social studies– or science-related informational texts are assets that support and enhance instruction but cannot replace specific content-area instruction.

2. *Choose Broadly.* Social studies and science are umbrella terms, and each includes a range of distinct disciplines. Therefore, instruction in each content area should draw directly from the fields that it represents (e.g., history, geography, physics, biology).

3. *Make Meaningful Choices.* Content-area instruction should be systematic and composed of meaningful activities constructed around big ideas—those foundational to the content area—that provide coherence throughout the curriculum. Texts should be a meaningful part of this enterprise. Therefore, for example, an informational book about spiders would be included because children were learning about how different animals' body structures and functions are related to their diet and habitat, rather than because they are learning about the letter "S" that week. That is not to say that teachers shouldn't make connections with

content children are learning in other areas of the curriculum—they should (e.g., *"Oh, everyone, look at this. 'S' is our letter of the week and 'spiders' starts with the letter 'S.'"*). Our point is that informational books intended to support content-area learning should be chosen and used in ways that promote children's learning of central aspects in *that* content area.

4. *Begin Early.* Content-area instruction should begin early and not be left to the upper elementary grades. There is substantial evidence that young children are far more competent to engage in discipline-specific learning than was previously thought.

5. *Emphasize Disciplinary Norms.* When instruction incorporates informational books that represent the cultural and linguistic conventions and norms used in specific disciplines (e.g., giving evidence to support a claim), it promotes not only the development of content knowledge but also children's interest and comprehension skills. Importantly, it promotes the ability to be a competent member of society, an "informed citizen" who can participate effectively in a shared culture (Hirsch, 2006).

   An example of a science norm shared among a community of scientists is the underlying premise of what science is. That is, current knowledge is just our best understanding of the evidence at the present time, rather than being a fact that is viewed as correct for all of time; knowledge gets revised with new evidence. Illustrations of this revision of "knowledge" include recognition that the Earth is spherical, not flat as once believed, and that the Earth orbits the sun rather than being the center of the universe. It is most likely that things we believe currently to be correct will be viewed in the same way as flat-Earth and Earth-as-center-of-the-Universe beliefs are today. *Developing an appreciation for the role of evidence over opinion or appearances* is a crucial component of a community with basic scientific literacy.

**6.** *Promote Accuracy.* When reading informational text, an important goal is for instruction to acknowledge and maintain the disciplinary integrity of the content area associated with the text. For example, discussion that focuses on the science concepts and reasoning presented in an informational book is necessary to support the authentic use of the text as an inquiry-related resource. This approach contrasts sharply with eliciting children's personal reflections and thoughts that spring from reading an informational book; this narrative approach to texts predominates currently in elementary classrooms (Norris et al., 2008). To illustrate, while reading an informational book about familiar, simple machines (e.g., *Playground Science;* Pitino, 2006), valuable discussion about a teeter-totter being a lever could include questions about what other everyday objects are levers (e.g., shovel, wrench) and talk about force—a central idea in physical science. However, if discussion stays on topics such as what playground equipment children like to play on most and which playground is their favorite, the opportunity to support disciplinary content is lost.

In closing this chapter, we offer the following questions for you to consider when deciding what trade books to include in your instruction:

1. What examples or applications of the big ideas (in social studies or science) that we have discussed in class are illustrated in the text?

2. How could this text help me foster connections between the big ideas and students' experiences?

3. What is the text's fit to national or state standards both for language arts and the content area that it addresses? And how does this text help meet specific goals that I have for both the content area (e.g., social studies, science) and the language arts curriculum?

4. Does the text address typical knowledge about a topic?

5. Does the text present opportunities to address knowledge that is important yet not very common (e.g., an oil spill) and therefore not likely to be encountered by my students?

6. What misconceptions or prior knowledge are my students likely to have on this topic and how does this text help me address them?

7. How could this text help me prepare my students for the next steps and topics in my curriculum?

8. How could the text facilitate connections to previous lessons?

9. How does this text connect to other texts that I plan to use in the curriculum? For example, connections could be made between an informational text that addresses animal camouflage (e.g., *Fish That Hide*; Swartz, 2000) and a fanciful story also about camouflage (e.g., *Hide, Clyde*; Benfanti, 2002) that is part of the prescribed reading curriculum.

## CHAPTER 4 APPLICATIONS FOR PRACTICE

### Try-It-On Activities

The following suggested activities require that you try ideas presented in this chapter in your classroom.

1. Analyze the dimensions of Book Genres, Quality of Content, and Quality of Illustrations to categorize the informational texts that you use (or plan to use) during a school year. Which books need to be replaced in or added to your curriculum?

2. Apply the selection questions at the end of the chapter to three informational texts you have used or plan to use in your classroom.

## FOR DISCUSSION AND REFLECTION

1. Quality and accuracy of content is essential in informational texts and yet often problematic (e.g., an average of one inaccuracy per book). How does a teacher choose texts that are developmentally appropriate and accurate? What do we know about young children's cognitive development that makes these choices critical?

2. How do informational texts help teachers and students meet new standards such as the Common Core Reading Standards for Informational Text K–5? Use the Reading Standards for Informational Text chart (p. 13) for K–2 at http://www.corestandards.org/assets/CCSSI_ELA%20Standards.pdf

3. What are some of the pros and cons of illustrations in informational texts? Discuss the important ways in which teachers have to evaluate illustrations and use them.

## HIGHLY RECOMMENDED WEBSITES

National Council for Social Studies' Notable Tradebooks for Young People http://www.socialstudies.org/resources/notable

National Science Teachers Association's Outstanding Science Trade Books for Students K–12 http://www.nsta.org/publications/ostb

# 5

# How Can I Use Shared Informational Book Reading in My Classroom to Build Children's Reading Skills and Background Knowledge?

In this chapter, we examine shared reading of informational books as a key interactional activity that involves you reading aloud to children and actively engaging them in talking about the text. Interactive shared reading experiences are vital in the early years of school because they provide opportunities for children to develop a number of important and inter-related literacy skills. These include the following:

- learning about the conventions of print,
- acquiring new vocabulary,
- becoming familiar with the structures of printed texts,
- comprehending and making meaning from texts,
- increasing background knowledge, and
- using texts as resources that extend learning beyond what is contained in the book.

Using shared reading to enhance young children's competence in one or more literacy skills is emphasized in different intervention programs, all of which highlight, to a greater or lesser degree, verbal, text-related interactions between the teacher and her students. As shown in Figure 5.1, some interventions focus on a specific set of literacy skills such as vocabulary knowledge (Beck & McKewon, 2007) or concepts of print (Justice, Kaderavek, Fan, Sofka, & Hunt, 2009). Other programs focus on improving children's skills in more than one target area and, therefore, include a variety of questioning strategies (e.g., Whitehurst, Zevenbergen, Crone, Schultz, Velting, & Fischel, 1999), retellings (Morrow, O'Connor, & Smith, 1990), and extending readings to other classroom activities (Wasik & Bond, 2001). As might be expected, given the dominant focus of stories in the early years of school, these interventions have been structured around readings of storied texts.

The positive effects on children's literacy generated by these shared reading programs have fueled an interest in

**Figure 5.1** Effective Shared Reading Interventions

| Program | Reference | General Focus | Instructional Focus | Strategies Used |
|---|---|---|---|---|
| **Text Talk** | Beck & McKewon (2007) | Vocabulary Development | Vocabulary instruction of targeted words after shared reading | Teacher: <br> • Uses the context of the story to define the word <br> • Provides a definition of the word <br> • Uses the word in other contexts <br><br> Children: <br> • Repeat the words <br> • Choose correct use of the word from examples <br> • Develop their own examples |
| **Print Referencing** | Justice, et al. (2009) Piasta, et al. (2012) | Concepts of Print | Systematic instruction of print knowledge | The teacher calls attention to four print domains: <br> • Print organization <br> • Print meaning <br> • Letters <br> • Words |
| **Dialogic Reading** | Whitehurst et al. (1999) | Oral Language | Conversational open-ended strategies of varying complexity | The child is asked to: <br> • Complete a sentence from the story <br> • Recall information from the story |

*(Continued)*

Figure 5.1 (Continued)

| Program | Reference | General Focus | Instructional Focus | Strategies Used |
|---|---|---|---|---|
| | | | | • Wh- questions (What, Where, Why)<br>• Distancing (extending information beyond the story to child's other experiences) |
| **STaR (Story Telling and Retelling)** | Karweit (1989)<br>Karweit & Wasik (1996) | Concepts of Print<br>Comprehension<br>Integration of Reading & Writing | Story reading, discussion, and retelling | First Reading:<br>• Background information about the story<br>• Shared discussion vocabulary words<br>Second Reading:<br>• Children retell in groups and individually and discuss vocabulary, dramatize the story |
| **Shared Storybook Reading** | Morrow et al. (1990) | Comprehension<br>Story Structure | Prereading, reading, postreading discussion, retellings, and attempted readings focus on inferential thinking and reasoning about the text | • Asking questions, making inferences, and discussion before and after the shared reading<br>• Retellings using puppets to facilitate story production<br>• Opportunities for recreational reading from the classroom's library corner<br>• End-of-day sharing discussion about story events |

adapting interactional strategies for use while reading informational books (Kraemer, McCabe, & Sinatra, 2012; Youngs & Serafini, 2012). Therefore, before we turn to considering informational books and their use as shared reading resources in the classroom, we provide an overview of shared reading as a way to support early literacy and briefly discuss recent evidence about the benefits of this practice.

## SHARED READING IS FUNDAMENTAL TO EARLY LITERACY

Nearly three decades ago, the Commission on Reading's report *Becoming a Nation of Readers* highlighted the critical need to involve children in interactive *shared reading*, or reading a book aloud to a group of students. The Commission noted:

> The single most important activity for building the knowledge required for eventual success in reading is reading aloud to children. . . . The benefits are greatest when the child is an active participant, engaging in discussions about stories, learning to identify letters and words, and talking about the meaning of words. (Anderson, Hiebert, Scott, & Wilkinson, 1985, p. 23)

More recently, citing the alarming statistic that nearly 40% of U.S. fourth graders lack basic reading competencies, the National Early Literacy Panel's (NELP's) research synthesis restated that early literacy skills are fundamental to success in school and identified a comprehensive cluster of reading-related skills (NELP, 2008). These involve precursors to literacy, such as knowledge of the alphabet, phonological awareness, and phonological memory. They also include more advanced skills, such as fluency (i.e., being a fast and accurate reader of text) and reading comprehension strategies, such as monitoring one's understanding of what is read, questioning, and summarizing (Ambruster, Lehr, & Osborn, 2008; NELP,

2008). These central literacy skills are developed within shared reading instructional practices.

## Teacher Beliefs and Shared Reading Practices

Shared reading is an important classroom event that is well established during the early years of school. Classroom teachers recognize that reading books to young children is crucial and report that they regularly engage in read-alouds as part of their literacy instruction. Teachers recognize that children's literacy benefits in many ways from shared reading. For example, teachers readily point out that shared reading facilitates children's literacy development in many different ways, including the following:

- providing opportunities for understanding the conventions of written language,
- building vocabulary and background knowledge, and
- promoting familiarity with different types of texts. (Teale, 2003)

When researchers have asked about the types of strategies used during shared reading interactions to support and extend student learning, teachers report that they target specific competencies. Teachers also say they often use interactive discussions and scaffolding to promote their students' learning. Their practices include modeling or demonstrating appropriate behaviors, eliciting student input, providing hints to support children's efforts, and giving explanations that extend children's responses (Morrow & Brittain, 2003; Pentimonti & Justice, 2010).

Teachers' views of themselves as frequent and purposeful implementers of scaffolded, text-focused talk are often not matched by independent observations of what occurs during instruction. Often, preschool and early elementary teachers do not allocate enough time for interactions during the shared reading (Dickinson, 2001). Other times, teachers do not use the reading in ways that fully benefit children's literacy development but typically guide the discussion using a narrow range of conversational strategies. The strategies they use most frequently are simple vocabulary prompts such as *"Does anybody know what a ukulele is?"* and recall questions about the reading that call for one-word responses such as *"Harry likes everything except taking a what?"* (Beck & McKeown, 2007). This helps explain why, when responding to teachers' questions, students often circumvent the content of the text and ignore its relevance to the discussion. Children focus instead on the book's pictures and on sharing their prior knowledge on the topic.

Overall, the consensus seems to be that a large proportion of teachers of young children do not typically "approach book use in a carefully thought-out, intentional manner" (Dickinson, 2001, pp. 200–201), and they rely on a few, primarily low-level scaffolding strategies that do not foster children's meaningful engagement with texts (Pentimonti & Justice, 2010). Nevertheless, there are also considerable differences among shared reading practices used in the classroom. In an often-cited study by Martinez and Teale (1993), all teachers engaged their students in interactive discussion; however, the extent to which each teacher contributed to the discussion varied extensively from teacher to teacher. All teachers initiated more talk than their students, but some teachers talked substantially more than others. Although all teachers dominated the discussions, the ratio of teacher-to-student talk per topic ranged from 1.4:1 at one extreme to 13.2:1 at the other extreme (i.e., between about 1.5 times and 13 times more teacher than student talk). In addition, teachers differed considerably in the *types* of questions they asked and the emphasis they placed on different kinds of information from the text (e.g., implicit vs. explicit events, inferential information, evaluative statements, pictorial content, making personal associations). Importantly, teachers' ways of inviting the children to voice their ideas about the stories—as part of promoting understanding—were stable across four different texts. This stability suggests that during shared reading, teachers consistently focus on and model specific sets of strategies and exclude others. For example, some teachers focus on questioning children about explicit events and pictures in the story, whereas other teachers primarily call attention to the characters and the story structure. Moreover, other teachers target students' skills at locating and reacting to key information, and they even use the story as part of a broader curriculum plan that includes activities beyond the text but directly relevant to it (e.g., drawing, writing, math).

Thus, depending on the teacher, children may have markedly different experiences with texts that, over a period, steer learning along some paths but not others; not all paths, however, lead to success in reading (Martinez & Teale, 1993). Indeed, as we discuss in the next section, intervention studies show that children develop unique sets of skills in response to the instructional variations and shared reading strategies used by their particular teacher. Unfortunately, though, not all skill sets are likely to ultimately support the long-term goal of developing the competencies necessary for independent reading.

## LITERACY SKILLS SUPPORTED
## BY SHARED READING

The NELP (2008) report *Developing Early Literacy*, which examined a handful of teacher-led shared reading interventions (i.e., a teacher reading a book to a whole class of young children) and concluded that shared reading has modest positive effects on children's oral language and early reading and writing skills, has been criticized by many researchers (e.g., McGill-Franzen, 2010). The shared reading programs reviewed in the report did not represent a single intervention; they varied in terms of both the amount of time allocated to shared reading and the type of strategies (e.g., interactive vs. not interactive) that were emphasized. Other reviews of research on shared book reading in classroom settings concluded that interactive book discussions in the classroom have positive effects on children's print knowledge and oral language (Mol, Bus, & de Jong, 2009; Schickedanz & McGee, 2010). However, the effects of shared reading are not automatic; they depend on two factors:

- The **quality of interactions** that occur before, during, and after the reading over time. That is, children's literacy skills depend on the *consistent use* of questioning practices that encourage children to consider relevant information in the text and make meaning from it.
- The **quantity of interactions** during the book's reading and rereading. That is, the amount of shared reading experiences overall, as well as the *number of times* a book has been read or reread, offer opportunities for interactions that are increasingly thought provoking and complex.

Another consideration is how interactive reading supports children's reading comprehension, given that "skilled readers are good comprehenders" (Snow, Burns, & Griffin, 1998, p. 62). In particular, a variety of scaffolding strategies facilitate students' understanding of what is read to them and the meanings they take away from the books (Schickedanz & McGee, 2010).

Successful programs that systematically address comprehension have used questioning techniques that invite children to reason about and draw inferences from the text (Morrow et al., 1990; Wasik & Bond, 2001). This is not to say that other programs that emphasize literal questions (e.g., Whitehurst et al., 1999) or focus on concepts of print (e.g., Justice et al., 2009), or vocabulary knowledge (e.g., Beck & McKewon, 2007; Brabham & Lynch-Brown, 2002) should be abandoned. Although they may not directly influence children's meaning-making skills, these programs do improve other important literacy skills such as vocabulary knowledge that, together with background knowledge, are fundamental to comprehension (Shanahan et al., 2010).

Interactional practices that build isolated reading competencies, such as decoding, labeling, or learning new words, are helpful but are not sufficient for children to comprehend what they read. Children need to be actively engaged in understanding books as they read (Schickedanz & McGee, 2010). Therefore, the most effective way to support children's literacy development is to combine practices that increase *comprehension,* such as encouraging children to reason and make inferences, with strategies that are effective for building other important literacy skills (e.g., decoding, word knowledge, concepts of print, text structures).

## THE NEED TO FOCUS ON SHARED READING IN A RICH VARIETY OF DOMAINS

The lack of attention to reading comprehension noted in the NELP (2008) report is no small matter, especially considering that exactly 10 years earlier the National Research Council (Snow et al., 1998) noted that building understanding from text should be a key priority for teachers of young children. The report recommended that

> beginning in the earliest grades, instruction should promote comprehension by actively building linguistic and conceptual knowledge in a rich variety of domains, as well as through direct instruction about comprehension strategies such as summarizing the main idea, predicting events and outcomes of upcoming texts, drawing inferences, and monitoring for coherence. (p. 7)

Therefore, to promote comprehension, teachers should consider two points. First, shared reading discussions must teach students effective ways of thinking about and analyzing the text (e.g., understanding the main points, interpreting meanings, using the text to draw inferences, using questions to monitor and clarify understandings, extending beyond the text; see also Shanahan et al., 2010). Second, shared reading should include a wide range of informational books to support the development of background knowledge that is built not just on experiences with storied text but also from engagement with discipline-specific content. However, a significant barrier to children developing the kind of knowledge that is essential for making meaning from diverse types of texts is the limited instructional time allocated to important subjects such as social studies and science in the early grades.

Social studies educators have issued serious cautions that the virtual elimination of the social studies curriculum has severely restricted opportunities for children to develop fundamental knowledge about the social world and acquire a sense of their own role in it. American students' performance on national and international tests indicates gaps in their knowledge of history, geography, and civics (Brophy & Alleman, 2009). This, in turn, constrains their ability to engage in meaningful learning through questioning, evaluating, organizing, analyzing, and challenging informational sources, all of which are essential aspects of inquiry in social studies education and necessary skills for an informed society (Duplass, 2007; Monte-Sano, 2011; National Council for the Social Studies, 2012b).

Similarly, in science education there is growing recognition of the need to develop competence in science as inquiry, and a considerable body of work underscores the crucial role that language skills play in understanding and engaging with the content and processes of science. Indeed, reading and writing are important aspects of scientists' work (Goldman & Bisanz, 2002; Norris & Phillips, 2003). When informational science books are combined with opportunities for authentic science inquiry, they support children's development of shared knowledge (L. Baker & Saul, 1994; Ford, 2006). Also, constructing and communicating their knowledge provides children with additional avenues to gain familiarity with the language and norms that are used by scientists (Gee, 2004).

In the next section, we present more details about instructional practices that generate content-related interactions during read-alouds of informational books. In our work in kindergarten science classrooms, we were guided by evidence on successful interventions (referred to at the beginning of this chapter) to support discussion during read-alouds of informational texts. The texts were selected (using criteria addressed in Chapter 4) to complement science inquiry activities and were thematically organized into meaningful units (e.g., Life Cycles, Living Things, Force & Motion). The units and associated book selections have been published elsewhere (Scientific Literacy Project [SLP], 2009). In the following section, we outline important guiding frameworks that support specific interactional reading strategies and provide examples of how teachers have used specific strategies to support children's learning.

## Strategies to Use With Science-Related Informational Books

### Guiding Frameworks

Teacher-student *scaffolded interactions* around reading books is key to children's literacy. Scaffolding refers to a teacher's efforts to assist the development of competencies within the learner's zone of proximal development, or the range where learners require assistance but can be successful with that assistance (Vygotsky, 1978). It is tailored to children's needs at the moment so that they are not given more help than is necessary. Several complementary frameworks involving scaffolding provide the foundation for the purpose and likely effects of different shared reading strategies.

First, within his *Psychological Distancing Theory,* Sigel (1986, 2002) has focused on interaction strategies by which adults' cognitive demands prompt and stimulate children to "reconstruct past events, and/or anticipate the future, and/or assume alternative perspectives on the present" (Sigel, 1992, p. 438). At the lowest level, distancing strategies ask the child to label, define, observe, or recount information. At the next level, distancing strategies call for the child to describe similarities and/or differences, sequence, classify, estimate, or infer similarities and/or differences. At the highest level, distancing requests call for evaluating consequences, inferring cause-effect relationships, generalizing, transforming, planning, or creating alternatives. Using strategies at all three levels that are aligned with children's knowledge and skills facilitates their learning from informational texts; recall from Chapter 1 that the structures of informational text include description, comparisons/contrasts, classification, cause-effect relationships, and if-then sequences.

Second, Gallimore and Tharp's (2001) expanded view of *Means of Assisted Performance,* or components of scaffolded instruction, has drawn from a diverse body of theoretical and empirical work to identify strategies that support the development of young children's thinking and language abilities. Depending on the learner's needs, these strategies may require different levels of teacher support. For instance, explaining complex vocabulary may involve a range of strategies—from those that require more explicit support (e.g., defining the word within the book's context and giving additional examples) to those that place the responsibility on the child (e.g., providing opportunities for children to use new vocabulary in different contexts). Strategies such as instructing, modeling, providing feedback, questioning, and encouraging cognitive restructuring (e.g., rethinking, adjusting, and/or expanding previous knowledge) are important in supporting learning from texts.

Third, Meyer's (1993; Meyer & Turner, 2002) extension of parent-child scaffolded interaction to the classroom shows important ways in which teachers interact and attempt to promote understanding with many children. Scaffolding, in Meyer and her colleague's framework, is composed of a balance of different types of teacher-class discourse. Teacher discourse strategies that support children's cognitive development include those that negotiate meaning for students and strategies that transfer responsibility from teacher to learner. Other necessary teacher discourse strategies support students' motivation and socioemotional development (Meyer & Turner, 2002).

These frameworks support the rationale for the types and levels of prompts as well as the use of additional strategies (e.g., retelling rereading) that both have been used in the literature referred to in these chapters and that we have adopted in our work with science-related informational texts.

### Types and Levels of Prompts

Use a range of prompts before, after, and during read-alouds to actively engage children in the reading process. These prompts include the following:

- **Recall prompts:** ask what happened at various points in the story or a story sequence;
- **Repetition prompts:** ask children to repeat new words;
- **Open-ended prompts:** ask children to talk about an event or series of events;
- **Wh- prompts:** ask What, Why, When, and Where questions;
- **Completion prompts:** ask children to complete a sentence or a part of a sentence; and
- **Explanation prompts:** ask children to explain the text, make causal connections between two events, or draw inferences from the text.

As we show in Figure 5.2, prompts may vary in terms of the complexity of thinking that is expected from the child. Prompts used at various levels of complexity (e.g., simple prompts vs. higher-level prompts) expand children's discipline-specific vocabulary, knowledge, and thinking skills.

Initially, before children become familiar with the vocabulary and structure of a new text, simple prompts (e.g., *"What is happening in this picture?"*) support them learning vocabulary through labeling and describing information (Blewitt, Rump, Shealy, & Cook, 2009). Teacher talk that invites children to participate in the reading by calling on them to talk about what they already know about the topic is important, because it enables children to draw relevant connections between

**Figure 5.2**  Types of Prompts

| Simple Prompts *ask the child to . . .* |
| --- |
| • label<br>• observe<br>• show information |
| **Intermediate-Level Prompts *ask the child to . . .*** |
| • sequence events<br>• classify<br>• estimate<br>• describe and infer similarities and differences |
| **Higher-Level Prompts *ask the child to . . .*** |
| • evaluate consequences<br>• infer meaning (e.g., about cause-effect relationships)<br>• use the information to interpret events beyond the immediate context of the book<br>• think about alternatives |

different parts of the content. Later, as children become more familiar with the text content, more complex prompts may be used. These promote children's skills in sequencing events, inferring consequences, and extending information to new situations. For example, asking, *"What do you think would happen to polar bears if oil spilled from an oil tanker and killed all of the fish?"* requires that children apply what they know about food chains and infer that polar bears will likely starve if their food source disappears. In Figure 5.3, we show examples of prompts involving different levels of complexity that may be used with a text about the butterfly life cycle.

### The Benefits of Retelling

The use of retellings to increase oral language, comprehension, vocabulary, and understanding of story structure is central to many shared storybook reading programs used with kindergarteners (Karweit, 1989; Morrow et al., 1990). In Chapter 2, we showed that young children can understand and retell informational text on a variety of science topics after the text has been

**Figure 5.3**  Prompts Example

| Types of Prompts | Examples | Skills |
|---|---|---|
| Simple Prompts | Tell me, what do you see on this page? | Observing Describing Labeling Defining Using simple number skills |
| | Where are the caterpillars? | |
| | What is it called when the caterpillars come out of the egg? | |
| | What colors do you see on the caterpillar? | |
| | Caterpillars spend their day _____. (p. 5) | |
| | What is a chrysalis? | |
| | How many caterpillars do you see on this leaf? (p. 6) | |
| Intermediate- and Higher- Level Prompts | Why is the caterpillar on the leaf? | Making connections Sequencing Recalling information Comparing/ contrasting Extending the information Drawing inferences |
| | What happens when the caterpillar has grown into its full size? | |
| | Is the caterpillar the same size when it starts out and when it's ready to go into a chrysalis? | |
| | How does the caterpillar start out? | |
| | Do all butterflies grow the same way? | |
| | Do other living things grow and change the same way? | |
| | Why is the chrysalis green? | |

**Hatching**

When caterpillars hatch from their eggs they are very tiny. You have to look very carefully to find them. But they grow very quickly. Caterpillars spend their day eating leaves.

5

**Eating & Growing**

These caterpillars are busy chewing the leaves of the milkweed plant. In just two weeks the caterpillars grow into their full size. That's about 2 inches long.

6

**Pupation**

This caterpillar is fully grown. It stops eating, finds a good hiding place like a leaf or a twig, and attaches itself to it. It is now ready to pupate. Pupation is when the caterpillar transforms itself into a chrysalis.

7

**Chrysalis**

This caterpillar has turned into a chrysalis. A chrysalis is like a hard case that hides and protects the butterfly that is growing inside it.

8

read to them just once. However, our examples of children's retellings highlight the many opportunities that retelling affords for instruction. Gaining access to children's perceptions of what they have heard or read, and the questions and prior knowledge that the reading sparks for them, is an important instructional strategy. It gives teachers windows into children's background knowledge and experiences and provides an indication of what children are taking from the book. In this process, dialogue, prompts, and teacher scaffolding play an important role in guiding children's learning of new, technical vocabulary (e.g., lever), and familiar words that have a second, unfamiliar meaning (e.g., school). For example, statements such as " . . . *and then they [dolphins] go to school*" (see Chapter 2) and the question about how a dolphin's mother can recognize her own dolphin baby at school when *"all the dolphins [look] the same"* show that many children still have to learn this alternate meaning for "school."

### Rereading Informational Books for Different Purposes

Rereading the same book allows for different features of the text to be highlighted each time it is read. This may involve first reading the text for general meaning, before focusing on specific vocabulary. Stopping to concentrate on a particular word at the outset may lead children to forget about the theme, given that we can process only a limited amount of information at a time and that young children's processing capacity is especially easily overloaded (Paas, Renkl, & Sweller, 2003). Reading a book more than once also provides opportunities for teachers to move beyond developing vocabulary to address conceptual issues. For example, when reading *What Is a Lever?* (see Chapter 2), children could consider the question of whether a short lever is as good at lifting a load as a long lever is. A seesaw is probably familiar to most children and is also relevant to use in discussing predictions, reasoning, and thinking about how one could find out the answer. Therefore, one of the many benefits of reading this or similar books is that it can familiarize young children with central concepts in physics, such as force.

## How Young Children Benefit From Informational Books in the Classroom

We now turn to examples of how teachers have used the strategies in actual classrooms to enhance kindergarten children's literacy skills and background knowledge during science instruction. We offer these examples with the caveat (also noted in Chapter 3) that we do not advocate the use of informational reading resources as a substitute for the rich inquiry experiences that support science learning. Rather, our examples are intended to highlight the many ways that science-related texts can function as additional resources that support the development of rich literacy and content knowledge.

### Opportunities for Accessing Children's Background Knowledge

Informational texts not only build background knowledge but also provide many opportunities for the teacher to access what children know about a topic. The following excerpt (Mantzicopoulos, Patrick, & Samarapungavan, 2013) was associated with reading *What Is an Ocean?* (Hughes, 2005) and activities designed to introduce children to the idea of the ocean as a habitat for living things. In this excerpt, Ms. Cannon used questioning strategies to activate children's prior knowledge about aspects of the ocean as a habitat that sustains marine life. During the reading, children also defined new words and made connections to the salt-water aquarium in their classroom, which was intended to serve as a model of the ocean (but did not yet have any marine life in it).

| Ms. Cannon: | *Well, the story we're going to start out with is "WHAT IS AN OCEAN?" What is an ocean? . . . What do you think it is?* |
|---|---|
| Jesus: | *It's . . .* |
| Ms. Cannon: | *Here we go, what's an ocean?* |
| Jesus: | *When it has water . . . (inaudible)* |

| | |
|---|---|
| **Ms. Cannon:** | *Aha. The ocean has lots of water.* |
| **Dora:** | *And it has whales and sharks and pebbles and it has lots of fishes.* |
| **Ms. Cannon:** | *OK.* |
| **Iriana:** | (inaudible) |
| **Ms. Cannon:** | (acknowledging Iriana's response) *These are all true! Yes, Peter?* |
| **Peter:** | *And it got big waves* (makes wave motion with hands). |
| **Ms. Cannon:** | *Wow! Carla?* |
| **Carla:** | *Sharks! Fish!* |
| **Ms. Cannon:** | *We know a lot already! Eduardo?* |
| **Eduardo:** | (inaudible) |
| **Ms. Cannon:** | (teacher repeats child's statement) *There's fish in the ocean?* |
| **Eduardo:** | (agreeing) *Aha.* |
| **Ms. Cannon:** | (begins reading again) *"WHAT DOES AN OCEAN LOOK LIKE? AN OCEAN IS A HUGE AREA OF WATER." Huge. What does huge mean?* |
| **Children:** | *It means it's . . .* |
| **Ms. Cannon:** | *Please raise your hand. Patrick?* |
| **Patrick:** | *It means it's really big.* |
| **Ms. Cannon:** | *It's really big! Really, really, really big! When you look out over the water, you cannot see any land on the other side, because it's sooo big!* |
| | (resumes reading) *"THE OCEAN IS SALTY. AND YOU MAY FEEL THE SALT ON YOUR SKIN."* (says to the class) *Do you know any water in here that is salty?* (children raise their hands) *Where, Peter?* |
| **Peter:** | *Aquarium.* |
| **Ms. Cannon:** | *Our aquarium, yes, our fish tank. Those are special fish that live in salt water. Do we drink salt water?* |
| **Children:** | (in unison) *No.* |

## Opportunities for Learning
## About Letters, Sounds, Words, and Text Structure

Children are likely to focus on the pictures and to ignore the printed words during shared reading, unless you refer explicitly to the print (Evans & Saint-Aubin, 2005; Justice, Pullen, & Pence, 2008). Therefore, it is important to purposefully integrate instruction about concepts of print during read-alouds of informational books—something that cannot occur during individual silent reading. Programs designed to teach children concepts of print (see also Table 4.1) emphasize objectives across four instructional domains (Justice et al., 2009):

- *Print organization.* This includes children's awareness of the function of different parts of a book, such as its title page, table of contents, and glossary. It also addresses the roles of the author and illustrator or photographer.
- *Print meaning.* This involves children knowing that words have meaning within the context of a story (e.g., *"This word says butterfly."*).
- *Letters.* This involves children understanding that letters, and groups of letters, are written symbols for particular sounds.
- *Words.* Word skills include knowing that words that appear in familiar contexts (e.g., STOP printed on a red octagonal sign, SLOW on the road before a speed bump), and understanding that written words correspond to spoken words.

Calling attention to concepts of print with explicit statements during read-alouds is an important part of reading informational books aloud. This can be done with comments such as the following:

- The **illustrator** *is the person who took pictures of the jungle animals in this book.*
- *This book has a* **Table of Contents** *after the title page. The Table of Contents tells us some of the important things that*

*are in this book. It also shows on which page we can find each one of them. See, "pulleys" are on page 4.*

- *The **Glossary** shows us about many of the new words that are in this book. It tells us what they mean.*

Once students have built a common understanding of these features, you may wish to refresh students' knowledge by occasionally asking questions during the course of different readings.

Next, we show how Ms. Donnely engaged kindergarteners in thinking and talking about motion and gravity prior to the reading of *Force and Motion* (Ramirez, 2007). She also used this as an opportunity to review children's knowledge of the letter "M" (Mantzicopoulos, Smarapungavan, & Patrick, 2009).

**Ms. Donnely:** (inviting children to come to the rug area for the shared reading activity) *OK, boys and girls, let's come on over. Please push in your chairs. Gravity is pulling everybody down, right? And you are all moving right now, you are all IN MOTION!*

**Alex:** (jumping excitedly as she moves to the reading area) *We are in motion!*

**Ms. Donnely:** *Now, I have not finished the word this morning that I have written up here (points to big board with the letters OTION on it), and I want to write the word MOTION. I am missing the first letter. This just says OTION. I want this to say MOTION. What letter do I need to put right there?*

**Children:** *EM!*

**Ms. Donnely:** *Em! Because em says what?*

**Children:** *Motion!*

**Ms. Donnely:** *It says, What does the letter M say?*

**Children:** *MMM.*

**Ms. Donnely:**     *Very good.*

**Jorge:**             *Motion, it said it, motion!*

## Learning New Vocabulary

Informational books provide excellent opportunities for children to learn new vocabulary that they are not likely to encounter as part of their everyday experiences. The examples associated with the reading *What Is an Ocean?* (Hughes, 2005, in Mantzicopoulos, Patrick, & Smarapungavan, 2013), shown earlier in this chapter, illustrate how the teacher, Ms. Cannon, assessed children's existing knowledge of words such as "huge" and, on occasion, extended their contributions with additional examples (e.g., *Really, really, really big! When you look out over the water, you cannot see any land on the other side, because it's so big!*).

Another example comes from a lesson where Ms. Burke read *Science Is Everywhere* (Yu, 2006) with her kindergarteners (in Mantzicopoulos & Patrick, 2011). In the excerpt we show next, she took the opportunity to review the meaning of the word "dissolve" with the children, a word that was unfamiliar to them.

**Ms. Burke:**     (reads text that refers to sugar added to a pitcher of water) *"WAIT, WHERE DID THE SUGAR GO? DO YOU KNOW?"*

**Children:**       (inaudible) (raising hands) *It "zoved"!*

**Ms. Burke:**     (points to Maria) *What's the word?*

**Maria:**           *It dissolved!*

**Ms. Burke:**     *It dissolved!* (continued reading) *"THE SUGAR DISSOLVED IN THE WATER. WHEN SOMETHING DISSOLVES, IT MIXES COMPLETELY WITH ANOTHER SUBSTANCE."*

In their analysis of the vocabulary differences between narrative and informational texts for young children, Hiebert and Cervetti (2011) noted that the vocabulary of science-related books is novel and complex, and lends itself to "extensive discussions and demonstrations" (p. 18). Words may be thematically organized around small clusters of concepts, and it is important for students to discuss the meanings of words alone and in relation to each other. For instance, as we show in the next excerpt, words representing concepts such as *fast* and *far* are clustered in the text *Force and Motion* (Ramirez, 2007) around the meaning of *strong force,* whereas words representing slow movement and short distance are clustered around the concept of *gentle force* (in Mantzicopoulos et al., 2009). To engage children to think about these concepts during the reading, Ms. Donnely invited the children to discuss and make inferences about the outcome of different forces represented in the text's pictures:

**Ms. Donnely:** (reading) *"A STRONG FORCE WILL MAKE AN OBJECT MOVE FAST AND FAR. A GENTLE FORCE WILL MAKE AN OBJECT MOVE SLOWLY AND A VERY SHORT DISTANCE." OK, now, which ball* (pointing to one of the boys in the picture) . . . *the boy here in the blue and yellow, the ball he's kicking, or the boy in the red and black?* (continues reading) *"WHICH BALL WILL TRAVEL FARTHER?"*

**Children:** *The red and black, the red and black, the red and black.*

**Ms. Donnely:** *OK, raise your hand if you can tell us why the red and black.* (Several children raise their hands.) *Valeria?*

**Antonio:** (inaudible)

**Ms. Donnely:** *Valeria?*

**Valeria:** *'Cause he's pushing it harder!*

**Ms. Donnely:** *OK, and we can tell that because . . . ?* (points to picture)

| Valeria: | *He's pushing with the foot and it's in the back.* |
|---|---|
| Ms. Donnely: | *His foot is way back and it looks like he's running, doesn't it? And* (points to other picture) **he** *is just trotting alongside the ball.* |
| Kaleb: | *Slowly!* |
| Ms. Donnely: | *Yeah, he is kind of moving slowly. Right. But* **he** *is running and he's got his foot back* (motions) *and he is really going to put that foot forward and he is BOOM, he's going to hit that ball really hard. So this ball is going to go farther.* |
| Martha: | *And go right into the shoot!* |

## Developing Accurate Disciplinary Perspectives and Connecting Them to Children's Lives

Familiarity with the conventions of discipline-specific reading media provides an avenue for children to develop skills that are essential for learning about and appreciating each discipline. Use of written resources is critical not only for learning information and developing knowledge in specific content areas but also for understanding disciplinary methods (e.g., documenting and sharing new knowledge, revising knowledge; Monte-Sano, 2011). Discipline-specific reading and writing conforms to linguistic structures and norms that are very different from those of storied text. Engaging young children with nonfiction resources not only provides them with new tools for learning but also likely promotes their knowledge acquisition while building their understanding about the structure and functions of scientific reading, writing, and discourse.

Reading developmentally appropriate, high-quality informational science books can help children construct accurate views of what science involves, including asking questions about the natural world, making and recording predictions, and recording and communicating observations and conclusions. In the SLP, for example, kindergarteners read books that emphasized that science is all around them: "Science is in the kitchen . . . science is in the backyard . . . science is on the sidewalk" (Yu, 2006, pp. 2, 8, 12), and that children use science machines when they ride a bicycle, play on a teeter-totter, or travel down a slide (Pitino, 2006). Thus, science is something they all can engage in, rather than a dangerous activity practiced by strange people wearing white coats and working alone in laboratories, as is commonly portrayed.

In the next excerpt, we show how Ms. Tarkington, at the beginning of the year, used the text *Science Is Everywhere* (Yu, 2006) as an opportunity to introduce the children to the idea of asking questions, making predictions, and considering what they know as they think about a natural event (in Mantzicopoulos & Patrick, 2011). As Ms. Tarkington engaged children in the discussion, she reinforced their question-asking (*That's a great question! How does it melt and dry out?*). In addition, she used and defined technical vocabulary (*That's a good prediction, or a guess,* and *What else do you predict or guess?*) that the children had learned previously to guide their contributions to the text-related discussion.

| | |
|---|---|
| **Ms. Tarkington:** | (reads) *"SCIENCE IS ON THE SIDEWALK. IT RAINED YESTERDAY. PUDDLES COVERED THE CONCRETE. BUT LOOK AT THE CONCRETE NOW!"* |
| **Hanna:** | *It's dry!* |
| **Karen:** | *It's dry!* |
| **Ms. Tarkington:** | (reads) *"WHERE DID THE PUDDLES GO?"* |
| **Hanna:** | *They dried up!* |
| **Ms. Tarkington:** | *They dried?* |
| **Children:** | (gesturing and talking excitedly) |
| **Ms. Tarkington:** | *Oh! Brandon, can you repeat your question that you asked?* |

| | |
|---|---|
| **Brandon:** | *How does water melt?* |
| **Ms. Tarkington:** | *How does water dry up and melt away?* |
| **Brandon:** | *Yeah!* |
| **Ms. Tarkington:** | *How does it? That's a great question! How does it melt and dry out? Caleb?* |
| **Caleb:** | *With the sun!* |
| **Ms. Tarkington:** | *The sun, you think the sun has something to do with it? That's a good* prediction, *or a guess, Caleb! What else, Christopher, what else do you* predict *or guess?* |
| **Christopher:** | *When the water is down on the ground, the sun makes it be hot and then the water goes down and it goes down the drain.* |
| **Ms. Tarkington:** | *So, you think it drains away?* |
| **Christopher:** | *It does!* |
| **Ms. Tarkington:** | *That's a good guess, that's a good guess. Emily what do you think?* |
| **Emily:** | *When the rain . . . when it's raining, then the sun dries the water up!* |
| **Ms. Tarkington:** | *OK, you guys are saying some really good things. I hear a drain and I hear the sun. So, you guys had some good guesses!* |
| **Emily:** | *I guessed good!* |
| **Ms. Tarkington:** | *So, science, is science just in the classroom?* |
| **Children:** | *No, no.* |
| **Hanna:** | (gesturing with hands) *It's all over the world!* |
| **Ms. Tarkington:** | *It's everywhere, in the whole entire world. Good job!* |

## Closing Comments: The Importance of Fit Between Classroom Discourse and Text Genre in Shared Readings

In this chapter, we sought to establish the importance of class-room discourse as a way of strengthening children's literacy development and background knowledge when engaging with informational written resources. The excerpts shown in this chapter highlight that to be effective, classroom discourse around informational books needs to be sensitive to the content and practices of the discipline represented in the text.

Even though trends are that more informational pieces are included in basal reading programs, there is also evidence that the recommended instructional activities and strategies that accompany these pieces are often not appropriately matched to the disciplines represented in the texts. In science texts, the selections of important vocabulary words that are recommended to teachers as a focus for their vocabulary instruction conform to narrative rather than informational frameworks. In an example provided by Hiebert and Cervetti (2011) about a text on tracking hurricanes, the instructor's guide recommended that teachers focus the discussion on words such as "shatter" and "destruction," rather than "anemometer," "meteorologists," or "satellite." However, technical words such as these are important for comprehending the scientific ideas presented in the text and are unfamiliar to many elementary school children. Without explicit attention to technical vocabulary, children are unlikely to build the conceptual connections needed for comprehending and learning from the text.

In addition, there is little attention to inquiry-oriented discussion that might accompany the basal reader selections and that would be appropriate for social studies or science instruction. Regardless of content area, the most commonly recommended discussion strategy involves questions on the readers' personal responses to the readings—not on a critical evaluation of the material (Norris et al., 2008). To be sure, in science-related readings about magnets, questions such as *"Have you ever used a compass to find your direction in an unfamiliar place?"* or *"What tricks can you do with magnets?"* are appropriate for teaching in any subject because they encourage students to connect their prior knowledge and familiar experiences with the content that is to be learned (Norris et al., 2008, p. 788). However, to serve inquiry-related roles in science learning, texts must be accompanied by instruction on the targeted scientific concepts and processes through discussion and activities that engage students' reasoning and provide opportunities for exploration, evaluation, and revision of their understandings about the world.

## CHAPTER 5 APPLICATIONS FOR PRACTICE

### Try-It-On Activities

The following suggested activities require that you try ideas presented in this chapter in your classroom.

1. Using a recording of a shared reading, identify and evaluate the types of prompts that you use to scaffold student understanding of an informational text. What types of prompts were most frequent? What was the quality of the students' responses? What proportions of prompts were at the simple, intermediate, and higher level as suggested in Figure 5.2?

2. Create a planned series of prompts to use with an informational text. What types of prompts are planned? How are the prompts sequenced? What proportions of prompts are at the different levels (i.e., Figure 5.2)? What do your choices say about how you use prompts to help students understand?

3. Compare Activity 1 and Activity 2 in terms of your experiences and the students' responses? How were they similar? Different? What role did the choice of text and the planning of prompts make?

## FOR DISCUSSION AND REFLECTION

1. Reflect upon and discuss the quality and quantity of shared reading interactions in your classroom (see these definitions in the section titled "Literacy Skills Supported by Shared Reading"). How would you describe your questioning techniques and the amount of shared reading experiences in your classroom? How does your questioning help students focus on the information in text? How often do you engage your class in shared reading? Do you reread books?

2. Discuss how important retelling and rereading are in your classroom and provide a rationale for their continued or increased use.

3. How do your practices prioritize the following benefits of informational texts in your classroom?

   - Accessing background knowledge
   - Learning about letters, sounds, words, and text structure
   - Learning new vocabulary
   - Developing accurate disciplinary perspectives that connect to children's lives

   What other benefits do informational texts offer your students?

## HIGHLY RECOMMENDED READING

Duke, N. K. (2004). The case for informational text. *Educational Leadership, 61*(6), 40–44. Retrieved from http://www.ascd.org/publications/educational-leadership.aspx

Oregon Literacy Plan. (n.d.). *K–12 teachers: Building comprehension in the Common Core.* Salem: Oregon Department of Education. Retrieved from http://www.edweek.org/media/24information-haveyouever.pdf

# 6

# How Can I Incorporate Writing With Informational Books?

In the previous chapter, we discussed how the benefits associated with reading informational books can be extended by engaging children in purposeful and strategic discussions of the books' contents. Writing is another important curricular area that can be paired with reading informational books. We use the term *writing* to cover a broad range of ways to communicate and physically represent ideas or meanings, including drawing, using symbols, dictating and/or copying words, and writing text; this is same way that writing is defined within the Common Core State Standards (National Governors Association Center for Best Practices [NGA] & Council of Chief State School Officers [CCSSO], 2010).

In this chapter, we briefly review reasons for why writing should have a strong presence in early elementary classrooms and evidence indicating that it usually doesn't. We then address ways to develop young children's nonnarrative (e.g., informational) writing skills while using informational books in content areas such as science and social studies. We show examples of how teachers can extend themes from informational text to include discipline-specific, nonnarrative writing. Our examples come from our work with kindergarteners learning science.

## WRITING IN THE EARLY ELEMENTARY GRADES

Reading and writing are crucial parts of communication and central components of literacy. Although some foundational elements of language are common to both reading and writing, other skills are just specific to writing (Shanahan, 2006). Therefore, children need explicit instruction in learning to write and plentiful opportunities for practice.

### Writing Supports Learning to Read

The process of learning to write helps children develop their reading skills (Abbott, Berninger, & Fayol, 2010; Conrad, 2008; Gerde, Bingham, & Wasik, 2012). In fact, both extended writing and summary writing are better at increasing children's reading comprehension than the commonly used practice of having children answer questions about the text (Hebert, Gillespie, & Graham, 2013). Early experiences with writing build language skills that are specific to writing, as well as skills needed for both reading and writing (Shanahan, 2006). Specifically, when young children are practicing writing, they

- develop *phonemic awareness,* or the ability to identify the sounds that make up words;
- gain *orthographic knowledge,* or how words are represented visually or spelled; and
- *integrate* phonological and orthographic knowledge, or link the sounds of words with their spelling.

Because phonemic awareness is an important component of reading, children who are learning to read usually receive considerable instruction in phonics. However, writing plays an important role in developing children's phonemic awareness (Gentry, 2005). Also, the children benefit more from systematic phonics instruction as their writing skills increase (Vernon & Ferreiro, 1999).

Integrating phonological and orthographic knowledge is another important component of being able to read. The process of thinking about how to spell words or identify the beginning or ending letters of words, as occurs when children try to independently write words, strengthens the association of *phonemes* (i.e., sounds) with the letters that represent those sounds (i.e., *graphemes*). Interestingly, kindergarteners' use of invented spelling—where children attempt to spell words as best they can and receive assistance and feedback specific to their development—is more effective at promoting reading skills than is specific training in phonological awareness, even for children in literacy-rich kindergartens (Ouellette & Sénéchal, 2008; Ouellette, Sénéchal, & Haley, 2013). Invented spelling is also more effective than phonemic training for kindergarteners who are at risk for reading difficulties (Sénéchal, Ouellette, Pagan, & Lever, 2012). The superiority of developmentally supportive invented spelling compared with phonics instruction for building reading skills may be because children's efforts to spell words develop both their phonemic awareness and their orthographic knowledge, in addition to supporting the *integration* of the two.

Writing helps develop orthographic knowledge, or knowing how words are spelled, and this makes reading comprehension considerably easier (Apel, 2009). When this knowledge is just emerging, children must devote substantial concentration to translating letters into sounds or sounds into letters, and this uses significant mental processing. Because people have limited cognitive resources to concentrate, think, and remember, thinking about how words are spelled reduces the mental resources that are available for actually comprehending the text (McCutchen, 2006). However, once written words are recognized automatically, people's minds are freed up to focus on the meaning of the text.

In a similar but reciprocal way, reading assists the development of writing. However, as we have noted already, children need specific instruction in writing to become competent readers and writers; reading instruction alone is not enough (Shanahan, 2006). Importantly, though, learning to read and learning to write complement each other.

## Writing Facilitates the Development of Other Skills and Knowledge

With instruction and repeated practice writing, children develop the fine motor skills needed to hold a pencil firmly but not too tightly, and to press hard enough to make clear marks without making holes in the paper. They also develop their visual and spatial orientation skills, which are necessary to form letters correctly (e.g., *"Which side of the o does the 1 go to make a b?"*), position letters *on* the line, and place sufficient space between the words.

Another result of instruction and considerable experience writing independently is that children's foundational transcription skills (e.g., handwriting, spelling) become automatic (Graham & Harris, 2000). This automaticity is necessary for children to write fluently; once the *form* of writing becomes automatic, more of the writer's thinking can be devoted to the *content* of what is being written (McCutchen, 2006). Therefore, improvements in handwriting and spelling lead to increased quality of children's writing (Berninger et al., 2002; Graham, Harris, & Fink, 2000; Puranik & AlOtaiba, 2012). Writing researchers recommend that elementary students receive daily writing instruction, beginning in kindergarten (Vander Hart, Fitzpatrick, & Cortesa, 2010).

Writing is a skill that is foundational to disciplines beyond English language arts. As we noted in Chapter 5, the way that language is used varies among subject areas. Therefore, literacy is "an essential aspect of disciplinary practice, rather than a set of strategies or tools brought in to the disciplines to improve reading and writing of subject matter texts" (Moje, 2008, p. 99). In addition to communicating content knowledge (i.e., *what* is known), language communicates *how* and *why* we know things within the discipline. Therefore, learning to write within a content area involves learning the ways of thinking and reasoning that make up that discipline (Monte-Sano, 2010).

Just as children's writing skills improve with practice, so do their views of writing and themselves as writers become more positive. As we noted in Chapter 3, when we discussed children's interest in reading, enjoyment increases with improvements in reading ability (Wigfield & Eccles, 2002). As with reading, children value and enjoy writing more as they are able to write more easily. Attitudes and motivation for writing are important to cultivate, because they lead to children spending time writing and taking care, paying attention, and putting in effort while writing, all of which contribute to writing achievement (Graham, Berninger, & Fan, 2007; Troia, Harbaugh, Shankland, Wolbers, & Lawrence, 2013). It is of concern, then, that children—especially boys—generally do not like writing and see it as considerably less enjoyable than reading (Graham, Berninger, & Abbott, 2012; Troia et al., 2013). These attitudes are believed to result from children having fewer opportunities to write than read, and from writing being emphasized less and holding lower status in early elementary classrooms compared with reading (Vander Hart et al., 2010). Therefore, researchers of writing argue that children will develop more positive attitudes about writing when it receives greater emphasis in the early school years than it does currently (Cutler & Graham, 2008).

## Opportunities for Writing

Considerably less attention is usually paid to young children's writing than to reading in the United States, despite writing being crucial for educational and occupational success as well as for everyday life. This imbalance in literacy instruction results in children having insufficient instruction and practice in writing during the early school years, which comes with serious and long-term consequences for individuals and society in general (Cutler & Graham, 2008). The most recently available, nationally representative writing achievement scores show that only a minority of U.S. students are proficient in writing. Only about one third of fourth graders write well enough to meet classroom requirements (Cutler & Graham, 2008). The situation is similar in middle and high school: just 27% of eighth graders and 27% of 12th graders have mastered all grade-level writing skills (National Center for Educational Statistics, 2012).

Within the small amount of time allocated to writing in the early grades, a sizable portion—about half—does not involve children writing connected text. Teachers spend about half of instructional time teaching basic writing, or *transcriptional*, skills, such as "spelling, grammar, capitalization, and punctuation" (Cutler & Graham, 2008, p. 915). Although these are necessary skills, as we discussed in the previous section, transcription skills alone will not produce many of the benefits that come from meaningful and connected writing. Researchers argue that for students to develop sufficient writing ability, they must spend more time writing connected text than they do currently (Cutler & Graham, 2008).

## INFORMATIONAL WRITING

The underemphasis of writing in the early elementary years is especially striking when it comes to informational or expository writing (Cutler & Graham, 2008). A sample of first-, second-, and third-grade teachers from across the United States reported the different kinds of writing activities their students engaged in. Most teachers assigned writing stories (96%) and worksheet exercises (86%); however, only a little more than half (59%) had their students engage in informational writing. Informational writing was particularly scarce in first grade— present in only 36% of classrooms. Because having opportunities to learn and improve leads to skill development, there is general agreement that the "difficulty that intermediate grade students display is related to their usually complete lack of practice reading and writing informational text" (Tower, 2003, p. 32). Therefore, literacy experts recommend that children have many opportunities to engage in writing expository text (Cutler & Graham, 2008).

Expository writing is well within the capabilities of young children. Despite having few opportunities to write in different genres during the early school years, children understand genre. Even young writers recognize that writing may serve different functions or purposes (Wollman-Bonilla, 2000). They show this understanding by using different genres (e.g., fictional, informational, or persuasive text), depending on what they wish to communicate and why and to whom. Differences in their use of genre-specific writing style or conventions are routinely recognizable during kindergarten and first grade, even though the children are just developing their writing skills (Donovan, 2001; Kamberelis, 1999).

## Concerns About Insufficient Opportunities for Informational Writing

There are a number of important concerns that stem from children's limited engagement in nonnarrative writing during the early school years. These transcend worries about inadequate writing skills in general.

1. *Adults write factual text most often.* Regular daily life requires that adolescents and adults write factual or informative text more often than any other genre. The summaries, reports, requests for information, or responses to others' requests—whether needed by educators, employers, employees, professionals, or friends—do not usually call for fictitious or inventive prose, but rather for clear information presented in a conventional form. Further, standardized assessments in all subjects are increasingly using expository writing to measure student learning. Therefore, educational

and occupational success depends on skills in composing nonnarrative text.

2. *Boys are especially disadvantaged.* Having limited opportunities for nonnarrative writing is believed to be especially detrimental for boys, who tend to write less, less often, and less well than girls and do not enjoy doing so (Graham et al., 2012; Troia et al., 2013). There is evidence, however, that although boys don't like writing fiction, they are much more interested if there is a *reason* to write. Therefore, just as reading informational books is seen as a way to increase boys' enjoyment of reading (see Chapter 3), so too is expository writing with an authentic purpose (e.g., communicating information to others, recording inquiries) believed to make writing more appealing to boys.

3. *Children do not write in content areas beyond language arts.* If children are not engaged in expository writing, or are doing so rarely, they will most likely not be writing in disciplines beyond the language arts, such as in science or social studies. As we have discussed already, the conventions of language are specific to each discipline and reflect the thinking and reasoning of that discipline. Content knowledge is expressed through language, therefore developing competence in a subject area involves coming to understand and use its linguistic conventions. Not having sufficient opportunity to develop writing skills in a content area undermines students' ability to think and reason in that discipline (Monte-Sano, 2011).

Concerns such as those just outlined have led to revisions of literacy standards. As we have noted already, the Common Core State Standards stipulate that children in the elementary grades be able to "write informative/explanatory texts to examine and convey complex ideas and information clearly and accurately through the effective selection, organization, and analysis of content" (NGA & CCSSO, 2010, p. 18). Therefore, the Common Core State Standards require early elementary teachers to engage their students in considerably more informational writing, and across a wider range of subject areas, than they do currently. In the next section, we discuss discipline-specific informational writing and reading activities as part of inquiry in history and science.

## PAIRING DISCIPLINE-SPECIFIC INFORMATIONAL WRITING WITH INFORMATIONAL BOOKS

Given the key role of audience, in that writing is generally intended to be read and understood by someone other than the writer, reading and writing are natural partners and are well-suited for integrated instruction. Through reading and writing students learn "how to access, interpret, challenge, and reconstruct the texts of the disciplines" (Moje, 2008, p. 100), and therefore come to understand content-area conventions of how knowledge is expressed and how its accuracy is questioned and evaluated. This occurs in the context of engaging in inquiry.

*Inquiry*, broadly defined as the process of asking questions, thinking about and evaluating evidence, and articulating and sharing one's understanding with others, is central to knowledge in each discipline. Therefore, engaging students in inquiry has become an important aspect of instruction in many content areas. When children document the inquiry process as they engage in it, many instructional objectives are addressed (see Table 6.1).

### Writing and Reading Historical Inquiry

Within history, inquiry typically involves examining documents (e.g., diaries, newspapers, records) or other artifacts from the past and getting eyewitness accounts. Timelines and family trees may be constructed as part of interpreting and displaying evidence. Evidence across a variety of sources usually shows that historical accounts vary depending on whom or where the information came from. Therefore, a central part of the inquiry process in history involves interpretation

| Table 6.1 | How Inquiry Enriches Children's Literacy |
| --- | --- |

1. Involves an authentic purpose for expository writing
2. Provides an authentic reason for reading informational books
3. Incorporates discipline-specific vocabulary
4. Introduces choice within the writing process
5. Enables differentiation of writing instruction matched to students' current skills
6. Involves discipline-specific forms of accessing, generating, recording, interpreting, and presenting knowledge
7. Promotes the understanding that knowledge is built from evidence and that evidence may be contradictory and requires interpretation rather than revealing simple, unchangeable facts

(Monte-Sano, 2011; Reisman & Wineburg, 2008). Understanding the past depends on interpreting information while contextualizing it—considering the sources of the information (e.g., the intentions and assumptions) within the time period (e.g., concerns of the time; Monte-Sano, 2010, 2011).

Informational books about history for children in the early grades appear to be less plentiful than those in other subjects. Nevertheless, there are excellent informational history and social studies books with content and language appropriate for kindergarteners and first graders that deal with topics such as immigration (Bersh, 2013) and neighborhoods (Wasta, 2010). Some books refer to the historical inquiry process. For example, before it addresses questions such as What would you eat? Would you go to school? and Was there time for play? the book *If You Lived When There Was Slavery in America* (Kamma, 2004) begins with a page titled "How do we know what it was like to be a slave?" (p. 8). Teachers can ask similar questions (see Chapter 5) while reading books that do not mention sources of information (e.g., *"How do we know what happened in those days?" "Do you think everyone who was there would say the same thing?"*).

Related to reading and talking about how we know about things in the past, children in the early grades may engage in historical inquiry of their own. For example, they could interview or ask questions—individually or in small groups—of people who lived through the same event (e.g., a local event or natural disaster), write about/record the eyewitness accounts, and then read the accounts to each other. Undoubtedly, some details will vary, which will require children to consider why some accounts of the event may be different from others. This develops a view of historical knowledge as complex, sometimes contradictory, and needing interpretation, rather than a straightforward account of predetermined factual information.

## Writing and Reading Science Inquiry

In this section, we illustrate some of the many ways that science notebooks can be used with young children while also presenting science inquiry and literacy activities. The examples we present of how teachers can include writing activities as part of inquiry science activities come from our work in kindergarten science classrooms. Our examples represent work produced from the first month of kindergarten through the end of the year.

Science inquiry typically involves asking questions, possibly making predictions, and, in the process of answering questions, making and recording observations, or drawing conclusions and sharing information with others. In the classrooms in which we worked, teachers focused on major themes in science (e.g., characteristics of living things, habitats, life cycles), and books and activities were related to those themes. Specific books that were read are shown in our project website (Scientific Literacy Project, 2009). We do not discuss the science content here; it is detailed elsewhere (e.g., Mantzicopoulos, Patrick, & Smarapungavan, 2013; Mantzicopoulos, Samarapungavan, & Patrick, 2009; Patrick, Mantzicopoulos, & Samarapungavan, 2009b; Samarapungavan, Mantzicopoulos, & Patrick, 2008; Samarapungavan, Patrick, & Mantzicopoulos, 2011). Writing activities were associated with books children had read and activities they conducted. Children wrote in individual science notebooks, which were loosely structured pages in a binder. At the end of a unit, pages were stapled together before being taken home to share with parents. These notebooks provided children with an authentic context for developing thinking and literacy skills (National Council of Teachers of English, 2004).

The science notebooks were very versatile in terms of individualizing learning, including meeting needs of English language learners (ELLs) and those with special needs. Therefore, they could be used by all children, despite the enormous variation that is typical within the early grades (Donovan & Smolkin, 2011). As we show in Figures 6.1 to 6.6, the notebook pages allowed considerable flexibility in how they were used by different teachers, at different stages of the year, and by children with varying levels of literacy skills within the same class. Children could keep records using whatever means were most appropriate in the context of their current abilities. For example, children could draw pictures or paste in photos. They could dictate and have an adult write for them and perhaps copy on top of or underneath the words. They could write their own words, using invented spelling or copying from a word wall, paste in words, or add check marks to charts. Children's entries were personal and did not need to be the same in terms of specific content or skills used; many different forms of recording promote literacy (National Association for the Education of Young Children [NAEYC] & International Reading Association [IRA], 1998). This flexibility enabled children with very different skills to all be successful at writing.

In terms of learning to write, children who were ELLs benefited from using the science notebooks. The loose structure allowed children to express themselves pictorially or in their first language while they were learning English, consistent with NAEYC & IRA (1998) recommendations. The notebooks afforded opportunities for these children to build on their understandings and to express what they knew, and also showed teachers what children knew and could do, without relying on verbal skills (NAEYC, 2003). The notebook entries were also used to encourage growth in children's verbal explanations, as we illustrate in some of the examples that follow.

## Figure 6.1  What is Science?

A. Making Predictions

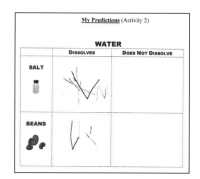

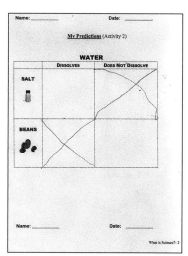

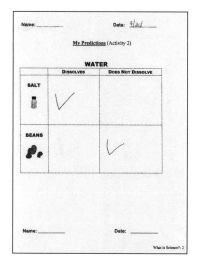

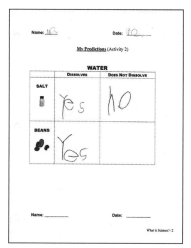

*(Continued)*

**Figure 6.1** (Continued)

B. Recording Observations

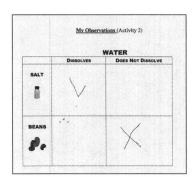

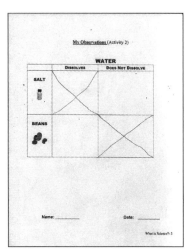

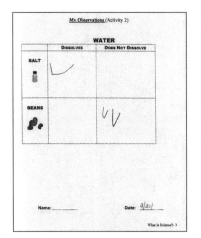

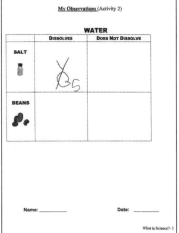

## C. Drawing Conclusions

Student dictated and teacher wrote: "Salt and this means it dissolved."

*What Is Science?*

At the beginning of the year, teachers introduced science by reading *Science Is Everywhere* (Yu, 2006). This book helps children understand that science involves answering questions about the world around them by giving familiar examples, such as puddles evaporating and lemonade mix dissolving in water. It also suggests simple investigations involving predictions and observations that children can conduct.

Each child conducted an investigation shown in *Science Is Everywhere* (Yu, 2006) to find out whether salt or beans dissolve when stirred in a cup of water. First, teachers modeled how to record predictions using a large chart and then children recorded their own predictions in the same chart printed in their science notebooks. At the beginning of the year, when kindergarteners' literacy skills are not well developed, we used pictures to accompany the words "salt" and "beans" on the charts and cups. The children needed only to make check marks on the charts. Next, children added salt to a cup of water, stirred it, and observed and recorded whether or not it dissolved; they did the same with beans. The examples in Figure 6.1 show a range of children's skills in recording their predictions and observations. One child obviously had great difficulty forming check marks, another two have written "Xs" or checks confidently, and a fourth has written the words "yes" and "no" in the chart. These charts enable students to compare their predictions and observations, with teacher assistance, illustrating the role of records in science. Finally, on a third page, children recorded the conclusions they drew, with the teacher's help, from the investigation. The examples of children's written conclusions reflect a broad range of writing skills. Two children dictated their conclusions to the teacher. One of these children drew a picture of herself stirring a cup of water and her dictated explanation, "Salt, and this means it dissolved," and the other child copied below the teacher's writing, "It tasted like salt." The additional three examples show more sophisticated pictures and words written only by children. One child drew a happy face beside salt crystals and a sad face beside beans, under the heading "Dissolves in [picture of water]"; he also pasted in a photo of the two cups. The other two children represented their conclusions more elaborately: they drew containers with water showing salt dissolved throughout the water in one and beans sitting at the bottom in the other, and added written explanations without teacher suggestions.

*Characteristics of Living Things*

Teachers and children read many informational books that discussed characteristics of living things, such as that they need water, air, and food. To review these features and relate them to themselves, children wrote a list of characteristics of living things. Children's differing skills in writing, and the inherent flexibility of the activity, is illustrated in the examples shown in Figure 6.2. The upper two notebook pages show the development of early writing skills. On the right, the teacher wrote the word "breathe" as dictated by the child. In the example on the left, the child copied two words from the list written by the teacher; we can see the difficulty the child had in placing letters on the lines. Both children also drew pictures of themselves. The lower two examples show more advanced writing skills. In the example on the lower right, a child copied all seven words from the teacher's list and then illustrated each one. In the fourth example, the child did not refer to the teacher's list but attempted to write the words himself, sounding out the letters. Even the most difficult of the words are recognizable—"xret" for "excrete" and "reprdus" for "reproduce."

In discussions, while reading books that referred to plants as being living things, children were encouraged to apply what they knew about living things (i.e., their characteristics) to plants. Because children are apt to think of plants' movement as a result of the wind, the internal movement of plants was demonstrated by having children place white flowers in clear and colored water. Children recorded their prediction of what two white carnations would look like after one was placed in regular water and the other in colored water. The next day they recorded the outcome, compared their predictions with observations, and discussed what the results showed. Examples of predictions and observations are shown in Figure 6.3. The examples again affirm that children can successfully record their thinking in ways matched to the development of their writing skills, within the same activity, because they could draw pictures and/or glue in photos, and, if they were able, write words.

**Figure 6.2**    Living Things: Applying the Seven Characteristics of Living Things to Themselves

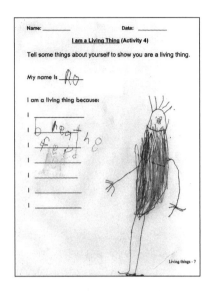

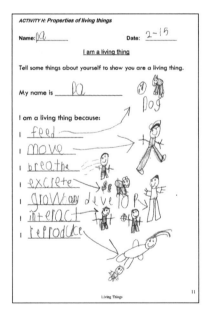

## Figure 6.3 Living Things: Living Things Move: Plants' Internal Movement

## A. Making Predictions

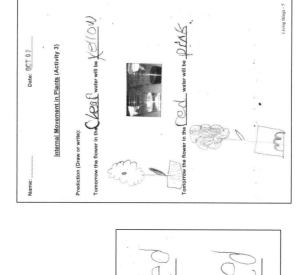

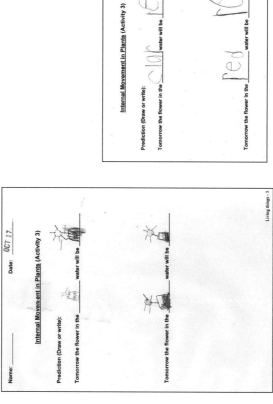

*(Continued)*

**Figure 6.3** (Continued)

B. Recording Observations

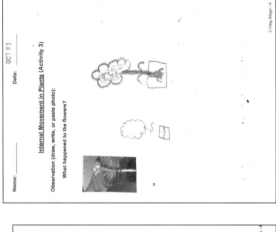

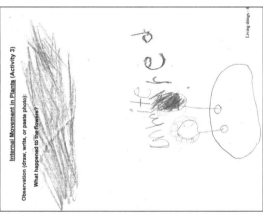

*Observations of Living Things*

Another writing activity that accompanied the books about living things involved children recording the living things they had seen on a walk with their teacher. Once inside again, children used a combination of words, pictures, and photos, depending on their abilities. Examples are shown in Figure 6.4A. The first example shows four photos (apples, butterfly, squirrel, and tree), taken by the teacher during the nature walk, just pasted onto the page. The next two examples show quite simple pictures—an insect, spiders, and a boy—with a teacher-written label on each. In one, the child copied the word "spider" below the teacher's. The child in the fourth example labeled photos of cattails and a squirrel, drew a tree, and recorded—fancifully—that he saw a bat. When children were to record observations, teachers emphasized that writing in science involves recording accurately what people see, rather than being imaginative with details. The notebook examples throughout this chapter show that children's depictions were typically realistic; however, the first example in Figure 6.4A—with smiley faces on the spider and insect—was an exception.

Books about living things addressed habitats (e.g., *Plants and Animals Live Here* [Wong, 2001]), and children were encouraged to record the different habitats of various living things. When reading a selection of books about the ocean, fish, kelp, and marine animals that live in a shell, children observed and wrote about the habitats of living things in their classroom aquarium. With a variety of living things to choose from, children could make choices about what to focus on—different kinds of fish, snails, crabs, an anemone, hermit crabs, a starfish, or a plant. Examples of their recordings, presented in Figure 6.4B, show many instances of invented spelling: the damsel fish swam "all ovr," the "uneamune" (i.e., anemone) moved on the rock, and the snails are "udrthe rodr" (i.e., under the rock) or "stdsnnthekornr" (i.e., stays/stands in the corner). We also see that children were still mastering placement of spaces between words and the use of lowercase versus uppercase letters within sentences.

**Figure 6.4**    Recording Observations of Living Things

A. Observations From a Nature Walk

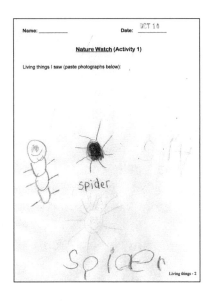

B. Observations of a Marine Environment (salt water aquarium)

Name: _____ Date: _____

Living Things in My Aquarium (Activity 4a)

What is it?

What does it do?

In which part of the aquarium does it stay the most? UP the RODR

Marine Life- 5

Name: _____ Date: __4-4—__

Living Things in My Aquarium (Activity 4a)

What is it? Hermit crab

What does it do? eatgoor lgge

In which part of the aquarium does it stay the most? bottom walks

Marine Life- 4

Name: _____ Date: __2-6__

Living Things in my aquarium.

What is it?

What does it do? move

In which part of the aquarium does it stay the most? aLLaRou nd

Name: _____ Date: __3-1__

Living things in my aquarium.

What is it? MD uheamJhe

What does it do? It moves

In which part of the aquarium does it stay the most? The rock

Name: _____ Date: _____

Living Things in My Aquarium (Activity 4a)

What is it? Swim FISH

What does it do? Sw_m, eat

In which part of the aquarium does it stay the most?

Marine Life- 1

Name: Lillith Date: APrl3

Living Things in My Aquarium (Activity 4a)

What is it? Snail

What does it do? StaShh he Korhr

In which part of the aquarium does it stay the most?

143

*Questions and Predictions About Living Things*

Within the context of posing questions about things they wanted to know and articulating predictions, the kindergarteners needed to learn what a question is and how it differs from a statement and a prediction. They did this throughout the year in the course of questioning, predicting, and making statements while reading and writing about science. In Figure 6.5, we show three examples of children's written questions and, in the lower left, a prediction. In the upper left example, a child dictated the question she wanted to know (i.e., How many wings do butterflies have?) and then copied some of the words underneath. This was written in the beginning of the school year, and she was learning to negotiate lines, spaces between words, and erasing. The other examples were produced later in the year and show more developed writing skills. The examples include instances when children used invented spelling (e.g., "elechrick eall," "chicins," "hahc"), placed spaces between words, numbered questions, overgeneralized punctuation (placing periods midsentence), and used uppercase letters within words ("cHicN"). The lower right example was written by a child who was still learning the difference between asking a question (i.e., of something he wanted to know about) and stating something he already knew (i.e., newly hatched chickens are wet).

*Observations About Life Cycles*

Teachers read books about life cycles in general and those of specific species (e.g., butterflies, chickens, penguins, frogs). Associated with these books were activities during which children could observe and record changes in live tadpoles, caterpillars, or chicken eggs—sadly, no penguins—that were growing in the classrooms. We show examples of children's notebook entries that documented the animals' growth in Figure 6.6. The entries were generally consistent with an informational genre: the pictures were realistic, with accurate coloring, labels, and dates, and without cute embellishments (e.g., smiles) that are typical of kindergarteners' drawings of

**Figure 6.5** Living Things: Asking Questions or Making Predictions

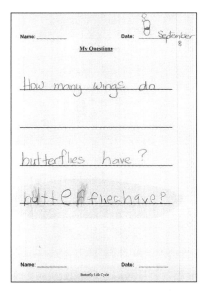

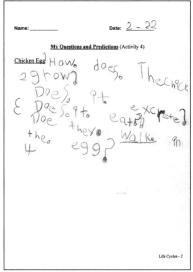

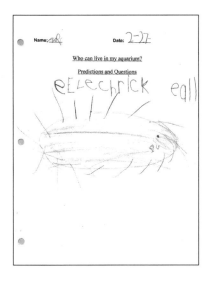

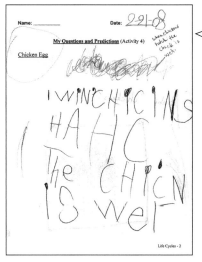

**Figure 6.6**    Living Things: Observing Stages of Life Cycles

A. Egg to Chicken

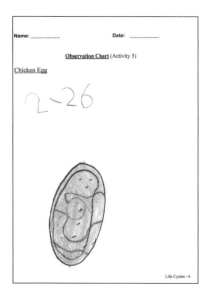

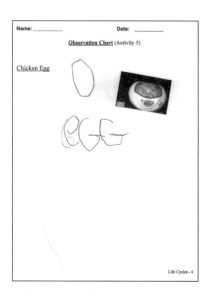

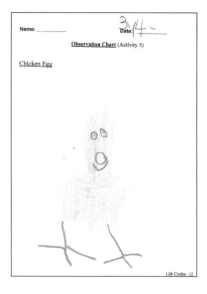

## B. Tadpole to Frog

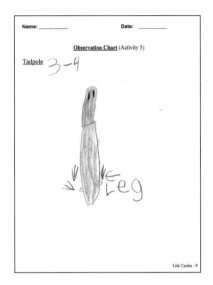

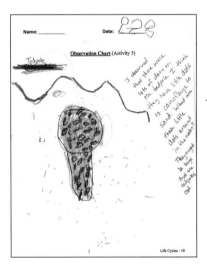

Dictated to teacher: I observed that there were lots of dots on the tadpole. I think they have little dots to camouflage to sand. What are those little dots around the water? They might be bugs that the tadpoles eat.

*(Continued)*

**Figure 6.6** (Continued)

C. Caterpillar to Butterfly

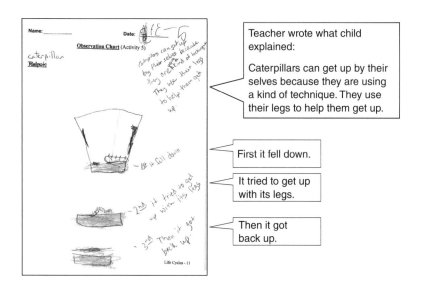

Teacher wrote what child explained:

Caterpillars can get up by their selves because they are using a kind of technique. They use their legs to help them get up.

First it fell down.

It tried to get up with its legs.

Then it got back up.

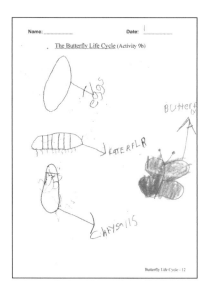

animals. The teachers emphasized that recording dates is a necessary part of tracking growth over time, and so children generally wrote dates on their observations—a feature of other notebook pages also. The first set of notebook examples shows children's documentation of a chicken's growth; we see what children saw when they used a scope to look inside chicken eggs, eggs in an incubator, and newly hatched chickens. The first example, recording the inside of an egg, includes blood vessels and accurate coloring and is a realistic likeness.

The second set of examples came from classrooms where children observed tadpoles. One drawing shows leg buds emerging at the back of the tadpole, which the child has pointed out with arrows and labeled. The second tadpole drawing is accompanied by quite detailed comments, including a clearly phrased observation (*"I observed that there were lots of dots on the tadpole"*), a feasible interpretation of the observation (*"I think they have little dots to camouflage [in the] sand"*), a question (*"What are those little dots around the water?"*), and a reasonable prediction (*"They might be bugs that the tadpoles eat"*). The teacher recorded this child's talk next to the drawing. This child also produced the notebook page in the final set of examples, which documented the butterfly life cycle. He made a series of drawings showing his observation of a caterpillar that attempted to crawl up the side of a container, fell down on its back (see its legs in the air), and struggled to get back up. Again, the teacher documented the child's explanations. The final page, with the full life cycle, shows the child understood the correct sequence of the stages and provided labels, although the cycle deviates from the norm in that it runs counterclockwise.

At the end of each unit, children took their science notebooks home to share what they learned with their family, which supports connections between school and home (see also Chapter 7). The notebooks served as records of children's progress throughout the year and reminders of concepts, vocabulary, and activities. Understandably, the children were very proud of their notebooks, and parents were usually delighted and often surprised at their children's learning.

The notebooks also supported assessment. They documented children's developing skills throughout the year, so they served as excellent records of changes in writing, vocabulary, spelling, and understanding. Therefore, they met recommendations to assess children's "strengths, progress, and needs" (NAEYC, 2003, p. 10) in appropriate and valid ways that were tied to their daily activities.

## In Summary

Informational writing is a natural partner to informational reading. It supports the development of both general literacy skills and subject-specific literacy practices that are authentic to content areas. Although there is considerable variability in young children's writing skills, writing activities can be framed so that all children—regardless of level of accomplishment—can be appropriately challenged and successful.

## CHAPTER 6 APPLICATIONS FOR PRACTICE

### Try-It-On Activities

The following suggested activities require that you try ideas presented in this chapter in your classroom.

1. Create a list of writing activities your students completed in the last four weeks (or which you are planning for the first four weeks of school). What types of writing are being experienced? What is the importance placed on writing in your classroom? Why?

2. Begin a daily informational notebook for a current area of study. Document the different types of writing that you observe in your students over several weeks. Investigate the different types of prompts that are successful for your students. For example, ask them to "describe," "predict," "sequence," and so on. Analyze their progress.

## FOR DISCUSSION AND REFLECTION

1. Carefully review the examples of kindergarteners' writing provided in this chapter. Discuss what these work samples illustrate regarding young children's informational writing, using the seven ways that inquiry enriches children's literacy listed in Table 6.1.

2. A core argument within this chapter is that young children are not provided with sufficient opportunities to learn to write in the primary grades. Discuss the barriers to these lost opportunities and strategies that could remove them.

## HIGHLY RECOMMENDED READING

Duke, N. K. (2010). *Informational text and young children: When, why, what, where, and how.* Retrieved from http://www.ngspscience .com/profdev/Monographs/SCL22–0469A_SCI_AM_Duke_ lores.pdf

Kletzien, S., & Dreher, M. J. (2004). *Informational text in K–3 classrooms: Helping children to read and write.* Newark, DE: International Reading Association.

# 7

# How Can Parents Use Informational Books to Support Children's Learning?

**A** great deal of children's learning happens during the everyday conversations and interactions that children have with family members. Parents can support and advance their children's school adjustment and achievement by talking with their children daily and reading books together (Fan & Chen, 2001; Patrick, Johnson, Mantzicopoulos, & Gray, 2011). Informational books are straightforward and enjoyable ways for parents to engage children in thinking, remembering, and learning about many interesting topics in a range of content areas.

In this chapter, we discuss children's access to informational texts at home and present reasons for why and how regular parent-child reading and conversations around the books play important roles in meeting children's thirst for new knowledge. We argue that parents can use the same interactional strategies at home that teachers use at school (see Chapter 5). These strategies, therefore, can be common tools that enrich children's learning experiences and provide continuity between home and school. Finally, we present examples of how teachers can guide and support parents' efforts to read and discuss informational books with their children. We recognize that, although we refer to parents, other familial caretaking adults such as grandparents, aunts, and uncles can and do take on the roles we discuss.

**PAUSE TO REFLECT**

1. Do your students have access to children's books at home?

2. Are your students' parents aware of differences across book genres?

3. How can you support greater parent awareness of the need to include informational texts when reading with their young children?

## SHARED PARENT-CHILD READING OF FICTIONAL VERSUS INFORMATIONAL BOOKS AT HOME

There is little doubt that today's parents receive numerous messages from many sources (e.g., the popular media, friends, teachers) that reading with children is vital for their children's success at school. Unfortunately, though, these messages do not usually communicate the value for children to experience a variety of genres. This may explain why, despite evidence for the benefits of reading informational books (see

Chapter 2), children have much fewer opportunities for reading these books at home compared with opportunities for reading fictional books (van Kleeck, 2003).

Contrary to what is commonly believed, children are more involved during shared parent-child reading when the book is informational than when it is fictional (Fletcher & Reese, 2005). When parents and children read *informational books* together, compared with reading narrative books,

- parents and children talk more and for longer periods of time;
- children ask more questions relevant to the book, relate the book's content to familiar knowledge or experiences outside of the book (e.g., *"Daddy's car rusted too"*), and refer to the book's content in the process of answering parents' questions (Pellegrini, Perlmutter, Galda, & Brody, 1990); and
- the parent-child talk involves more higher-level thinking and reasoning skills. Children make at least twice as many comments that involve inferences, explanations, and comparisons (Price, van Kleeck, & Huberty, 2009).

It is likely, too, that engaging with informational books fulfills children's intrinsic need for learning about aspects of the world—an issue that we discuss later in this chapter.

## Young Children Usually Have Little Access to Informational Books at Home

Even though young children find informational texts across many different topics to be extremely interesting and appealing (see Chapter 3), they usually have very few opportunities for reading this kind of book at home. To illustrate this issue, we refer back to the study we discussed in Chapter 2, where we considered young children's understanding of and interest in reading informational books. Although our study involved books on different science topics, there is no reason to think that the results would be any different if we had used informational books in other content areas, such as history or geography.

Recall that we read excerpts from four informational texts (shown in Figure 2.1, page 42) to kindergarteners and asked them to retell the content. We then asked children about their interest in the excerpts and whether or not they read similar texts at home: *"Do you read books or look at books like this at home or not?"* Many children told us that they didn't read informational books at home; the numbers varied depending on the topic of the book. Approximately half of the children said they read life-science books, like the ones about dolphins (53%) or ways that animals move (48%). Fewer children said they read books on science topics such as light (42%) or simple machines (32%).

As concerning as these statistics appear, they may well present an inflated picture of children's opportunities for reading informational texts. Adults often focus on the similarities between fictional and informational books and see them as interchangeable (Shymansky, Yore, & Good, 1991); it is quite likely that children do too. Therefore, many children who said they read informational books at home may well have been thinking of fiction with animal characters—realistic or fantasy—or fictional stories about machines or the sun. Opportunities for children to read informational books at home may be scarcer than our data suggest!

## Girls Are Especially Disadvantaged in Their Access to Informational Books at Home

Boys and girls retold the excerpts that we read to them equally well, and there were no gender differences in children's interest across the different topics (see Chapters 2 and 3). However, boys and girls had different opportunities for reading science-related informational books at home. We show this discrepancy, separately for girls and boys, between interest in reading books on different topics and their opportunities to do so (see Figure 7.1). Specifically:

- a little more than half of the boys, compared with one third of the girls, said they read books about life science at home;
- fewer girls than boys said they read nonbiology informational books at home;
- approximately half of the boys said they read books about the Earth or the environment, compared with one third of the girls; and
- even fewer girls (22%) told us they read books with physical science themes at home, compared with about 40% of the boys.

It is striking to see that many children are interested in reading informational books but do not have access to them at home. In particular, it is girls who are missing out on having their interests met—the differences between interest and opportunity are greater for girls than for boys.

**Figure 7.1** Boys' and Girls' Interest in and Access to Informational Books at Home

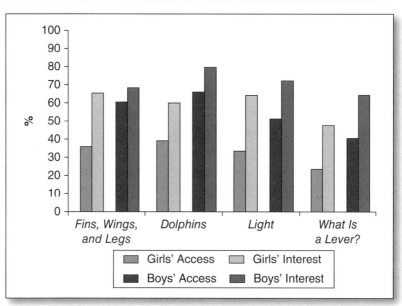

Considering that interest is strongly related to family and cultural expectations and opportunities to learn, this difference between girls' and boys' opportunities to engage with informational science books is not trivial. First, it helps explain the frequent finding that girls usually view science as less interesting and engaging than boys do (e.g., Miller, Blessing, & Schwartz, 2006; Patrick, Mantzicopoulos, & Samarapungavan, 2009a). Second, it provides insights into the underrepresentation of women in advanced classes and careers involving science, technology, and engineering—a statistic that most researchers believe is not related to low ability, but to cultural and social factors (Brotman & Moore, 2008; Eccles, 2007; Spelke, 2005). Therefore, the future ramifications for girls having fewer opportunities to read about science, and therefore fewer opportunities for developing interest in science, are significant. Researchers have argued that adults have considerable power to encourage girls' interest in science by exposing them to informational science books but, unfortunately and unintentionally, adults are mostly not fulfilling this role (Ford, Brickhouse, Lottero-Perdue, & Kittleson, 2006).

## READING INFORMATIONAL BOOKS AT HOME ADDRESSES CHILDREN'S CURIOSITY ABOUT THE WORLD

One of the characteristics of young children is their inherent curiosity and interest in the world around them—both natural and social. They seem to ask questions almost incessantly. When talking with adults, young children ask between 76 and 95 information-seeking questions per hour—an average of about three questions every two minutes (Chouinard, 2007, p. 99). These information-seeking questions reflect, first, children's ongoing thirst for knowledge and understanding and, second, their awareness that they have gaps in what they know and that there is additional knowledge to be learned (Kuhn, 2004). The information-seeking questions that children ask, and the responses they receive to these questions, have critical implications for the development of reasoning, language, and cognitive growth, as well as background knowledge. We elaborate on these implications in the following section.

Young children are especially curious about the natural world. An influential argument is that children have a unique, innately controlled tendency to seek information and learn about nature, broadly defined (e.g., humans, animals, plants, forests, rivers and streams, mountains, mud, mountains, swamps, forests, sunlight, clouds; Chouinard, 2007; P. C. Lee, 2012). Children's intrinsic interest in information about natural phenomena is reflected in the number and the types of questions that they ask. Below are typical examples of these questions, taken from studies by other researchers and ourselves (see Table 7.1).

| **Table 7.1** | Examples of Young Children's Information-Related Questions |
| --- | --- |

| **Life Cycles** |
| --- |
| *Why do babies have to be there* [in their mommy's tummy] *for so long?* (Callanan & Jipson, 2001, p. 31) |
| *Do the baby deer come out of an egg like the chickens do?* (Davis, 1932, p. 71) |
| *Does the baby calf come out of the mother?* (Davis, 1932, p. 71) |
| *Do babies come from eggs?* (Callanan & Oakes, 1992, p. 222) |
| *Do they look like little seeds* [in their mother's tummy]? (Davis, 1932, p. 71) |
| *What do they look like when they are in the mother?* (Davis, 1932, p. 71) |
| *When somebody dies, then, doesn't his heart beat?* (Przetaczink-Gierowska & Ligeza, 1990, p. 81) |
| *Does hair grow at night?* (Przetaczink-Gierowska & Ligeza, 1990, p. 80) |
| *What makes a cat have a kitten? Does it come from an egg?* (Przetaczink-Gierowska & Ligeza, 1990, p. 80) |
| *Why has a dead caterpillar grown quite small? When I die shall I also grow quite small?* (Piaget, 1955, p. 185) |
| *Why do people die?* (Perez-Granados & Callanan, 1997, p. 12) |
| *How do babies grow in your stomach?* (Mantzicopoulos & Patrick, 2012) |

*(Continued)*

**Table 7.1**  (Continued)

| Plants, Animals, and Humans |
|---|
| *How do bees eat?* (Przetaczinka-Gierowska & Legeza, 1990, p. 97) |
| *Why are the moths similar to the butterflies?* (Przetacznik-Gierowska & Ligeza, 1990, p. 78) |
| *Where do the cookoos live?* (Przetacznik-Gierowska & Ligeza, 1990, p. 78) |
| *Does the butterfly make honey?* [No] *But why does it go on the flowers?* (Piaget, 1955, p. 183) |
| *What makes the flowers grow in the summer?* (Piaget, 1955, p. 210) |
| *Why do the trees have leaves?* (Piaget, 1955, p. 235) |
| *Does the water you drink go to your legs?* (Callanan & Oakes, 1992, p. 219) |
| *Why does Daddy, James [big brother], and me have blue eyes and you have green eyes?* (Callanan & Oakes, 1992, p. 221) |
| *How do leaves fall off the trees?* (Mantzicopoulos & Patrick, 2012) |
| *Why [do] flowers come in the summer and not in the winter?* (Mantzicopoulos & Patrick, 2012) |
| *Why do our brains think?* (Mantzicopoulos & Patrick, 2012) |
| *Why do animals eat other animals?* (Mantzicopoulos & Patrick, 2012) |

| Earth and Atmospheric Science |
|---|
| *How is the rain made up in the sky?* (Piaget, 1955, p. 207) |
| *Why does it rain sometimes?* (Callanan & Oakes, 1992, p. 218) |
| *Why is it that the sun sometimes doesn't come out?* (Perez-Granados & Callanan, 1997, p. 12) |
| *Why can't we reach the sky?* (Perez-Granados & Callanan, 1997, p. 12) |
| *Where did all the water from in the lake come from?* (Callanan & Oakes, 1992, p. 219) |
| *Where does the sky end?* (Perez-Granados & Callanan, 1997, p. 12) |
| *What are the stars for?* (Perez-Granados & Callanan, 1997, p. 12) |

> *If somebody takes snow in the winter and puts it in a basement where it is cold, would it be there for a whole year, also in summer?* (Przetaczink-Gierowska & Ligeza, 1990, p. 81)
>
> *How big are the stars and the sun?* (Mantzicopoulos & Patrick, 2012)
>
> *What is the sun made of?* (Mantzicopoulos & Patrick, 2012)
>
> *How does the earth rotate?* (Mantzicopoulos & Patrick, 2012)
>
> *Where do the stars come from?* (Mantzicopoulos & Patrick, 2012)
>
> *What makes a tornado?* (Mantzicopoulos & Patrick, 2012)
>
> *How did the moon get there and why is it sometimes all the way round?* (Mantzicopoulos & Patrick, 2012)

Questions such as these enable children to collect information that explains things or events to them, or to find out about things beyond their immediate environments. The information children gather from grown-ups is purposefully and persistently sought, processed, and (re)structured to address what children think are gaps in their knowledge. Through this process, they piece together and construct their knowledge of the world. This includes adding new information to things they knew already (i.e., prior knowledge) and making revisions or adjustments, including fixing or eliminating inaccuracies in prior knowledge (Chouinard, 2007). Thus, information-seeking is a gradual process within which questions function as central tools that children use to advance their conceptual understandings by garnering knowledge available from others.

## INFORMATIONAL TEXTS IN CONJUNCTION WITH PARENT-CHILD TALK PROMOTES CHILDREN'S LEARNING AND MOTIVATION

High-quality, developmentally appropriate informational books are valuable resources for parents to use when addressing children's zest for learning about the world (however, see Chapter 4 for guidelines in choosing appropriate books). In addition to learning content presented in the books, children learn about finding answers to questions and even how to frame or articulate questions themselves.

The following is an excerpt of a conversation between David and his mother, prompted by an informational book about ducks and ducklings that Mrs. Lowery read to her kindergarten class. It illustrates many of the benefits of shared informational book reading paired with parent-child dialogue. The excerpt also shows how David's mom uses the conversation as an opportunity to meet David's request for more knowledge, by suggesting they read other books together.

**David:** *Do horse babies come from eggs?*

**Mom:** *This is a cool question! What do you think? Which animals hatch from eggs?*

**David:** *Chickens and ducks.*

**Mom:** *And horses? What do you think?*

**David:** *I think their mom makes them.*

**Mom:** *Yes, they are babies when they come out of their mom's body. Because some animals give birth to live babies. But some other animals lay eggs and the babies grow in them, in the eggs, outside of their mom, and they hatch when the baby is ready to come out.*

**David:** *When the eggs are outside of their mom, she watches them. That's what it [the book that his teacher read] said.*

**Mom:** *Yes, she does watch them, and makes sure they are warm so the babies inside them can grow.*

**David:** *How many babies can there be in an egg?*

**Mom:** *I think only one.*

**David:** *But in a horsie?*

**Mom:** *One or two. Maybe more. Maybe we can find a book about horse mommies and babies.*

In the excerpt, we see that David's mom's initial response— *"That's a cool question"*—communicates that asking about different animals' growth processes is interesting and worth learning about. Then, rather than just telling David whether or not baby horses hatch from eggs, she prompts him to consider what he knows about animals that do (i.e., connect his new question with what he already knows). This encourages David to mentally compare horses with chickens and ducks and venture a guess based on his existing knowledge, rather than ignore what he already knows. The excerpt ends with David's mother suggesting that they read another book to find out about baby horses, which is part of socializing him in culturally appropriate ways to find out what he wants to know.

The discussions that occur before, during, and after shared reading, triggered by a text's content, offer many benefits for children. Besides providing opportunities for children to develop and practice important literacy skills (see also Chapter 5), experiences with informational texts provide opportunities for parents to

- promote social interaction skills, social routines, and norms;
- support children's views of themselves as competent readers;
- extend children's motivation in topics they are already interested in;
- initiate children into using books or other resources for finding answers to questions; and
- guide children's language development and initiate them into ways of reflecting about and creating meaning from texts.

We discuss each of these points, and provide examples, in the sections that follow.

## Promoting Social Interaction Skills, Social Routines, and Norms

Read-alouds that involve interactions between parents and children offer opportunities for children to practice and establish important routines, such as handling and taking care of books and helping put books away at the end of the reading. Also, through participation in shared reading activities, children gain experience in reciprocal and cooperative interactions and improve social skills that are essential for appropriate behavior at school. Specifically, children learn to

- participate in a shared activity with an adult by responding appropriately to a parent's invitation to read together;
- engage appropriately in conversations initiated by the adult (e.g., react to a parent's comment during the reading with thoughts that are relevant to what is being read);
- initiate invitations to adults for reading books together, and begin and maintain joint conversations about the book;
- practice self-regulatory skills (e.g., learn to take turns during the book-related conversations);
- learn that it is okay to pause for a moment to think before responding to a comment or question; and
- experience a sense of satisfaction from doing things with others.

## Supporting Children's Developing Views of Themselves as Competent Readers

Children's beliefs about how competent they are at different activities develop while they engage in these activities. For example, experiences while learning to read influence children's views of how good they are at reading and how much they enjoy it (Aunola, Leskinen, Onatsu-Arvilommi, & Nurmi, 2002; Chapman, Tunmer, & Pronchow, 2000). Young children interpret experiences with academic content as being directly related to their ability to excel in a given area (e.g., *"I am a good reader because I read with my mom at home."*). Also, the types of activities that parents and children are involved with (e.g., reading books, visits to the library), as well as the amount of time that they spend on them, signal how important the activities are and influence children's motivation (Mantzicopoulos, Patrick, & Smarapungavan, 2013). Therefore, reading books frequently and talking about the books not only supports the development of reading skills, but also promotes children's beliefs that they are good readers and that reading is important.

## Extending Motivation in Topics of Interest and Sparking Interest in New Areas

Opportunities for conversations that are intended to provide direction to children's information-gathering create a fertile ground for them to learn from informational text. The interactions around reading informational books can be a productive way to explore and gain new knowledge, particularly when it occurs in response to children's interests—as manifested by requests for more knowledge on specific topics. For instance, a child's question *"Mommy, how does the sun stay up there?"* may prove a fruitful opportunity for a parent to respond to her child's requests by engaging the child in reading and discussing topic-specific information: *"Mommy isn't really sure about that. It's a great question, though. I am sure we can find a book that can help us learn about the sun."* Informational printed resources, when used in a collaborative context with knowledgeable adults, may help children fill gaps in their knowledge and provide additional opportunities for parent-child dialogue on topics of interest. Interests are also fueled by information—with increasing knowledge come new questions, while interest withers when new learning does not occur (Renninger, 2000). Even a simple question, when taken seriously, can grow into an enduring interest (e.g., marine life, the solar system, geology, robotics, Native Americans, the Civil War).

As we noted in Chapter 3, research on young children's motivation for reading different types of genres shows that reading informational books with elementary school students can enhance children's motivation for reading. Many children—more often boys—are not interested in fiction, or "things that are not true," and therefore, because fiction pre-dominates, do not find reading particularly satisfying or inter-esting (Newkirk, 2000). However, these children usually discover that reading for knowledge and having their curiosi-ties about the physical or cultural worlds explained energizes their interest in reading (Guthrie, Hoa, Wigfield, Tonks, Humenick, & Littles, 2007).

## Initiating Children Into Texts as Cultural Tools for Finding Answers to Questions

In addition to sharing their own ideas on a topic, adults may respond to children's questions by introducing them to a variety of learning resources, including informational books. With guidance from adults, children gradually learn that questions may be examined in different ways (e.g., first-hand explorations vs. learning from others) and that knowl-edge may be constructed from many sources. For instance, to address children's questions about leaves, parents may decide to read a children's book, in addition to watching a television program, visiting a park or a relevant exhibit, or telling what they know. In this way, parents may support their children's ongoing interest by introducing them to informational texts as tools in the process of gathering and sharing information.

## Guiding Language Development and Initiating Children Into Ways of Reflecting About and Creating Meaning From Texts

Information tools, used in the context of scaffolded discus-sions between children and grown-ups, become part of and transform the child's structures of understanding and think-ing about the world. Indeed, when asked to read an informa-tion book with their children, parents engage in many interactions that help develop children's language learning and knowledge construction (Pellegrini & Galda, 2003; Pellegrini, Galda, Jones, & Perlmutter, 1995). For example (see also Table 7.2), parents facilitate children's understandings through statements that

- support children's understanding of grammatical conventions, including exceptions to the rules (e.g., *"It sounds like it should be 'sheeps,' doesn't it? For most words we put an 's' on the end when there are more than one, like 'pig' and 'pigs.' But some words stay the same whether there is one or a lot of them. There might be one sheep or lots of sheep."*);
- build and reinforce vocabulary knowledge (e.g., *"Nutrients are like vitamins that help us stay healthy and grow," "Plankton is a group of very tiny plants or animals that float on the water"*);
- provide focus on relevant information (e.g., by asking the child to identify and label objects in a book, by helping a child describe the purpose of objects);
- illustrate the reasons for relations between objects or events (e.g., *"The sun helps the flower grow," "A blossom is the flower part of a plant"*);
- promote classification skills (e.g., *"It says here that mammals give birth to their babies. Mammals are born alive, they don't hatch from eggs. How many animals can you think about that are mammals? How many animals that are not mammals?"*);
- build connections between the child's knowledge and the new information in the text (e.g., *"This page says that you can find these birds around marshes and ponds. Do you remember the bird that we saw in Celery Bog? It was a Heron! We have these birds here in our back yard!"*);
- help the child extend knowledge beyond the text (e.g., *"What other birds live in bogs?," "What sorts of insects other than bees do we see in our garden?"*);
- promote knowledge of print and conventions of print (e.g., by running a finger along the words while reading, by asking questions about the sounds of specific letters, by asking the child to recognize specific words); and

- promote number skills (e.g., *"How many times do you see the word 'seeds' on this page?," "How many different plants did we see in this book?," "Can you see more sharp spines on the cactus or more thorns on the rose bush?"*).

In light of the focus on early parent-child reading, there are many benefits for helping parents use reading strategies similar to those that we discussed in Chapter 5, along with reading more books that are informational. In the next section, we present ways that teachers can help support parents' use of interactional strategies during shared reading of informational texts. These suggestions piggy-back onto approaches suggested for use by the teacher in the classroom so as to provide continuity between children's home and school.

## ALIGNING HOME AND SCHOOL INFORMATIONAL BOOK READING PRACTICES

The many potential benefits of parent-child reading and associated conversations are increased when these activities are aligned with the school curriculum. Supporting parents to engage at home with their children in activities that are similar to or build on what children are doing at school provides continuity in children's experiences. This is particularly important for students from cultural or linguistic minorities, who are more likely to experience discontinuities between home and school in terms of the content and patterns of discourse, routines, preferences, and expectations compared with children in the majority culture (Gallimore & Goldenberg, 2001; O. Lee, Fradd, & Sutman, 1995). These incongruities are believed to contribute to many young minority students feeling uncomfortable at school and uncertain of what is expected from them. Therefore, it is critical to address the interface between home and school by helping parents understand how practices in schools promote their children's learning and what they can do to support their children (O. Lee, 2002).

Efforts to forge home-school connections can take many forms. However, a crucial element involves providing parents with resources (e.g., books) that match those used in the classroom. The goal of such alignment efforts is to provide parents and teachers with shared sets of tools (e.g., same types of books) and interactional strategies (e.g., questions), which parents can use as they interact with children across a variety of formal and informal learning activities. This enables parents to see what children do and learn at school, and children can engage in the same kinds of activities in both contexts, thus developing greater continuity between home and school. Additionally, parents can make concrete connections (e.g., share other examples) between the materials provided by the school and examples from their own culture(s)—connections that may be beyond the scope of the teacher's knowledge or experience. We next discuss examples of materials we developed for children to bring home from school, designed to foster home-school connections.

## Examples of Materials Teachers Can Use to Involve Parents in Reading Informational Books at Home

Engaging parents and children in shared reading activities centered on informational books is a nonthreatening avenue to promote home-school continuity and parent-child talk about content areas, in addition to strengthening children's literacy skills. Therefore, as part of a recent collaboration with kindergarten teachers to integrate science instruction with literacy, we developed a set of home resources to complement the classroom activities (Mantzicopoulos et al., 2013). The home activities were coordinated with the science book reading activities that teachers used in the classroom. Our goal was to develop a set of common materials that parents and teachers would use to read, write, and talk about science with children. Weekly home activities were designed to do the following:

- actively engage children and parents in reading informational science books;
- encourage parent-child communication about science and school, through providing the same books for home as were read in the classroom; and
- build parents' skills to engage in science-related conversations with their children during everyday routines.

Furthermore, given that children brought their science notebooks (see Chapter 6) home from school at the end of each unit, these notebooks also aided home-school communication.

*Training session.* In training sessions, we introduced parents to the same conversational reading strategies that teachers employed (see Chapter 5) so that parents could use these strategies at home. We showed short clips of specific shared reading strategies. In addition, we provided parents with a sheet that outlined helpful prompts (Figure 7.2) and included examples of how these prompts may be used while reading a book about the life cycle of a butterfly.

## Home Materials

We developed a set of home materials for each of the 20 weeks of the classroom activities. In those weeks, each child took home a packet of materials in a plastic sandwich bag with the project logo and the child's name on it. A sample is shown in Figure 7.3, and we discuss its contents next.

*"Dear Family" letter.* A short letter, signed by the classroom teacher, briefly outlined the key activities that the children were involved in during the week and provided one or two suggestions of what parents could ask their children about school. The presentation of the letter was simple, with large type and attractive pictures, to encourage parents to read it.

*Informational book.* A copy of an informational book that the children had read with their teacher during the week was included in the packet. Children could keep the book.

| Figure 7.2 | Parent Handout With Examples of Conversational Reading Strategies |
|---|---|

**Eating & Growing**

These caterpillars are busy chewing the leaves of the milkweed plant. In just two weeks, the caterpillars grow into their full size. That's about 2 inches long.

**Pupation**

This caterpillar is fully grown. It stops eating, finds a good hiding place like a leaf or a twig, and attaches itself to it. It is now ready to pupate. Pupation is when the caterpillar transforms itself into a chrysalis.

**Chrysalis**

This caterpillar has turned into a chrysalis. A chrysalis is like a hard case that hides and protects the butterfly that is growing inside it.

**Open-Ended:**
- Tell me, what do you see in this page?

**Recall Prompts:**
- How does the caterpillar start out?
- How long does it take for these caterpillars to grow to their full size?
- What happens when the caterpillar has grown to its full size?
- What is the chrysalis like?

**Labeling:**
- What is the name of the plant that the caterpillar is on? (milkweed)
- What is it called when the caterpillar is ready to transform itself? (pupation)
- What do we call the hard case in which the butterfly grows? (chrysalis)

**Making Comparisons:**
- Is the caterpillar the same size when it starts out and when it's ready to turn into a chrysalis?

**Thinking Critically:**
- Why do you think caterpillars look for a good hiding place when they are ready to pupate?
- Why might it be helpful that the chrysalis is green?
- Do other living things grow and change the same way?

*Science book reading record and stickers.* As a way to encourage parents and children to read the book regularly—three to four times during the week—and a way for families

**Figure 7.3**    Sample of an Informational Book Home Packet

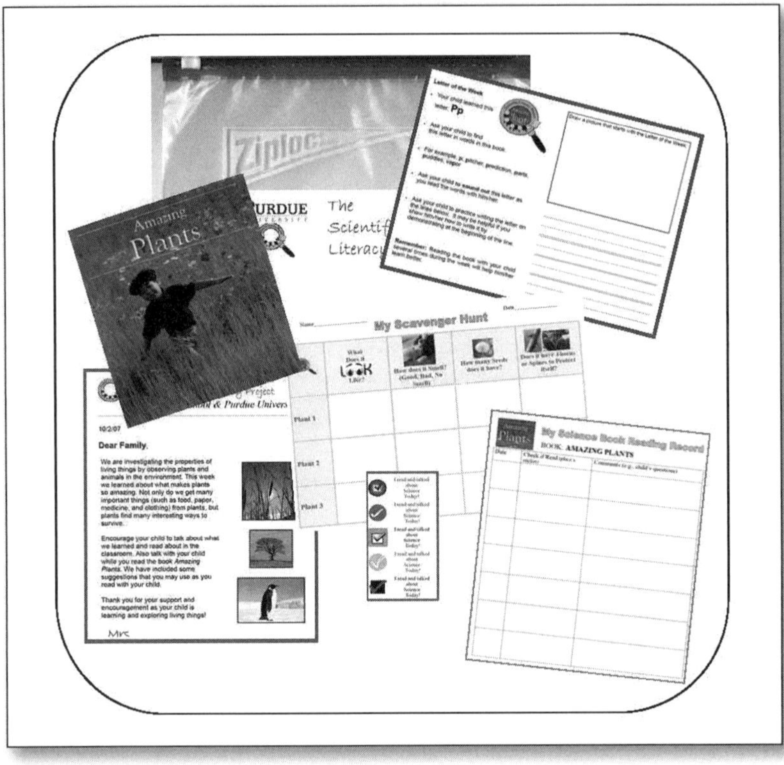

*Source:* Book cover from Santiago (2006).

to keep track of their reading, we supplied a recording sheet in each weekly packet. Additionally, we provided stickers for children to attach to the record sheet each time they read the book (see Figure 7.4 for examples of completed record sheets). There was also space for parents to record the dates they read the books each week as well as make comments about the book reading, including children's questions or comments. These records serve as a means for parents to provide feedback to teachers and to inform teachers of what they do at home to support their child's learning—an important aspect of a partnership.

*"Let's Read Together and Learn Science" sheet.* To facilitate the use of different conversational strategies, we provided an

**Figure 7.4** Sample Science Book Reading Record Sheets

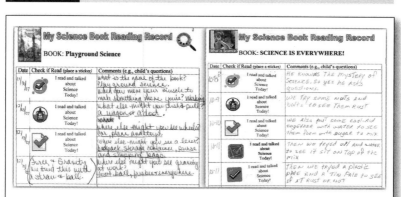

Book cover images from Pitino (2008) (left) and Santiago (2006) (right).

insert with each book, containing suggestions of different types of questions parents could ask as a way of supporting parents' developing familiarity with the conversational book strategies. The insert (an example of the front page is shown in Figure 7.5) included a list of vocabulary words as well as questions to support children's numeracy skills. Additional items included with each insert were "Explore and Discuss Questions" (e.g., *"I wonder what would happen if . . ."*) and suggestions for simple activities that parents and children might engage in during the course of the day (e.g., observing and describing the different plants that children would encounter in their immediate environments—home, school, a park, the supermarket). These strategies and support materials can be easily shared by teachers during the regularly scheduled parent-teacher meetings.

*Activity sheet.* Additional activities (e.g., My Scavenger Hunt) related to the book's theme were included in the home packet. These activities provided suggestions for parents and their children to explore and talk about science during the course of the week.

*Letter of the Week sheet.* Children in the kindergarten classrooms in which we worked focused on learning a different letter of the alphabet each week—the Letter of the Week

**Figure 7.5**    Book Insert

# Let's Read Together and Learn about Science

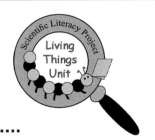

Scientific Literacy Project

Living Things Unit

## Amazing Plants

### by Rosario Ortiz Santiago

......................................................

# Helpful Reading Ideas

### To Get Started:

**Discuss the cover page:**

- What do you think this book is about?
- Which living things will we read about?

**Read the title and author to your child. Review the table of contents.**

- What does the table of contents tell us?

**Ask your child to identify each picture.**

### While Reading:

Run your finger from left to right under each word as you are reading to your child. As you read, discuss the book with your child. For example, ask:

**Page 1:**

- What important things do people need in order to live?

- What do plants need for growing?

**Pages 6–7:**

- What are some other insects that spread pollen? Think of insects you've seen around flowers.
- Is there a plant that you think stinks? Maybe a kind of vegetable or fruit?

**Page 12:**

- What do you predict a deer would do if it tried to eat a cactus?

### When Finished:

Look again at pages 7, 8, and 12. Ask your child to name each plant and to think of one or more ways in which the plant protects itself.

- How do plants spread their seeds?
- Why do some plants smell good and others smell bad?
- What fruits can you think of that have seeds?

The century plant spends most of its life looking like a short, spiky cactus. But, once every 25 years or so, it blooms with flowers

### Number Skills

Use the book to strengthen number skills. For example ask:

- How many times do you see the word "seeds" on page 4?
- How many different plants did we see in this book?
- Can you see more sharp spines on the cactus (p. 12) or more thorns on the rose bush (p. 9)?

### Words of Science

Review these new words with your child, talk about their meaning, and use them in examples during the week.

| | |
|---|---|
| amazing | blossom |
| air | wind |
| survive | pollen |
| animals | cactus |
| grow | odors |
| seeds | smell |
| stem | insect |
| nutrients | oxygen |
| cotton | shelter |
| soil | thistles |
| attract | stink |
| chemical | rash |
| protect | oil |
| thorns | spines |
| desert | spongy |

.......................

### Science in Action

**The same/ different**

**Record what I see**

**I still don't understand why...**

Photos from iStock.com.

(LoW). We created the LoW sheet and included it in the home packet to create a link between the LoW and the book the children took home. The LoW sheet identified the letter that the children were taught in their class that week, listed words from the book that included the letter of the week, and contained space for children to both draw a picture of something beginning with the LoW and practice their handwriting skills. In the spring, when teachers had finished teaching individual letters and were introducing children to sight words, the LoW was replaced by the Word of the Week.

## Effectiveness of Parent-Child Information Book Reading and Conversations for Children's Learning

After 20 weeks of the home information-book reading program, there were a number of important differences between the children who did and those who did not participate in the home information-book reading program, despite there being no differences at the beginning of the program (Mantzicopoulos et al., 2013). Compared with their peers, children who read and talked about science books at home with a parent scored higher on a standardized test of science knowledge (i.e., they developed more broad background knowledge), believed they knew more about science, and said that, when it came to learning science, their families were more helpful, supportive, and encouraging.

We were interested to find out whether parents read and talked with their children differently as a result of participating in the home program. Therefore, we examined how parents read informational science books with their children at the end of the program, comparing parent-child participant pairs with parent-child pairs who did not. This involved looking at video recordings of 40 parents reading the same, previously unseen informational book (*Life Cycle of a Bean;* Royston, 1998) with their child. Half of the parent-child pairs had received weekly packets containing an informational science book and suggestions for talking about and doing science related to the book's content. The 20 other children had been read informational science books in their classroom throughout the year but did not receive materials for use at home.

Parents who participated in the home book reading activities—compared with parents who did not—read with

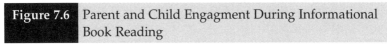

**Figure 7.6**   Parent and Child Engagment During Informational Book Reading

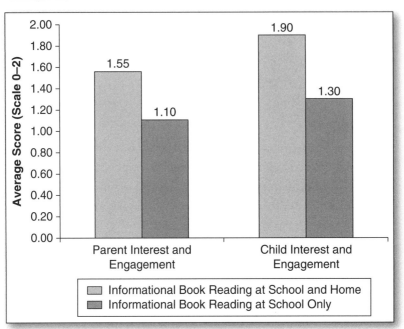

more expression, were more engaging, and more attentive to their child's comments or reactions to the text. Also, their children were more interested and engaged during the reading compared with children not in the home program. These comparisons are shown in Figure 7.6.

We also examined parents' use of a variety of book-reading strategies during reading *The Life Cycle of a Bean*. These strategies were as follows:

- Attends to features of the book prior to the book reading
- Accesses the child's prior knowledge prior to the book reading
- Asks closed-ended questions
- Asks open-ended questions
- Scaffolds participation through comments and book-related behaviors such as pointing to pictures
- Scaffolds connections between the reading and children's experiences

- Draws attention to sounds of letters or words
- Draws attention to text in general by running finger through words and sentences
- Draws attention to new words and defines them
- Acknowledges and responds to children's questions or comments
- Uses the text to support children's mathematical knowledge (e.g., by counting objects, by paying attention to relative size or shapes of objects)

Parents who participated in the home book reading activities spent more time reading and talking about the book while reading, compared with parents not in the home program (see Figure 7.7). Also, they used more of the reading strategies; we show these comparisons in Figure 7.8.

Not only did the home-program parents use a greater variety of reading strategies, but each one of the strategies

**Figure 7.7** Reading Time and Scaffolded Dialog Strategies

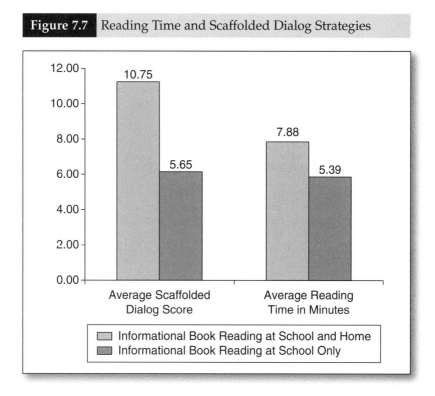

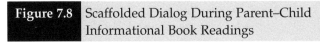

**Figure 7.8** Scaffolded Dialog During Parent–Child Informational Book Readings

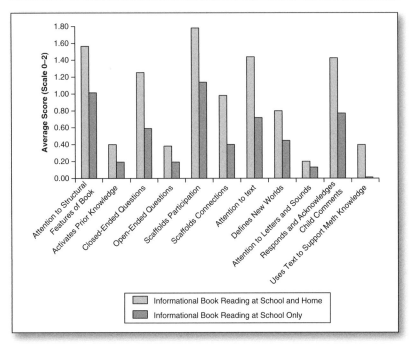

was used more often by this group, compared with parents who were not in the home program. In Table 7.2, we show examples of specific strategies that these parents used to support their kindergartener's learning of science, reading, and mathematics.

**Table 7.2** Excerpts of Parent -Child Readings

| Typical Examples of Scaffolded Parent-Child Talk During Informational Book Reading |
| --- |
| 1. **Attending to structural features of the book prior to the book reading**<br><br>• Drawing attention to the book's title<br>• Asking about the author (e.g., *"What does the author do?"*)<br>• Pointing to the table of contents (e.g., *"This tells about what's gonna be in this book."*) |

### 2. Accessing the child's background knowledge prior to the book reading

<u>Ernest and his Dad</u>

| | |
|---|---|
| **Dad:** | (points to photograph on book cover) *Do you know what this looks like?* |
| **Ernest:** | *Beans!* |
| **Dad:** | *What kind of beans?* |
| **Ernest:** | *Lima beans?* |
| **Dad:** | *They sort of look like lima beans, don't they?* |

<u>Eduardo and his Mom</u>

| | |
|---|---|
| **Mom:** | (looks over title page with Eduardo) *What do you think that you're going to see in the book?* |
| **Eduardo:** | *Beans, how they're born.* |
| **Mom:** | *How what is born?* |
| **Eduardo:** | *The bean.* |
| **Mom:** | *What are beans? What do you think beans are?* |
| **Eduardo:** | *Beans.* |
| **Mom:** | *They are beans, but what are they?* |
| **Eduardo:** | *Um, they're small balls that we can eat.* |
| **Mom:** | (reads) "BEANS ARE SEEDS THAT GROW IN PODS. WE EAT MANY KINDS OF BEANS INCLUDING KIDNEY BEANS, BLACK-EYED PEAS, AND FAVA BEANS." |

### 3. Asking closed-ended questions

<u>Christopher and his Mom</u>

| | |
|---|---|
| **Mom:** | *We don't want to kill the ladybugs, do we?* |
| **Christopher:** | No! |

<u>Gus and his Mom</u>

| | |
|---|---|
| **Mom:** | *Have you seen a field of beans before?* |
| **Gus:** | *Yeah.* |

*(Continued)*

**Table 7.2**    (Continued)

---

**4. Asking open-ended questions**

Jennifer and her Mom

| Mom: | (reads) "INSECTS COME TO DRINK THE NECTAR." *What kinds of insects do you think come to drink the nectar?* |
|---|---|
| **Jennifer:** | *Bees* (pause), *and caterpillars, and butterflies?* |

Cara and her Dad

| Dad: | (Dad had read the segment about bees collecting pollen on their hairy legs.) *What if they didn't have hairy legs? Would it still work?* |
|---|---|
| **Cara:** | *Mmmmm.* (not a yes or no sound) |
| **Dad:** | (laughing) *Maybe not so good.* |

---

**5. Scaffolding participation through comments and book-related behaviors (e.g., pointing to pictures)**

Michael and his Mom

| Mom: | *What are these?* (points to picture of different kinds of beans) |
|---|---|
| **Michael**: | *Black-eyed beans.* |
| Mom: | *And these are fava beans.* (points to picture of fava beans) |

James and his Mom

| Mom: | *It's growing, isn't it?* (points to picture of bean; James nods) *Yeah, that's the bean. It grew out of it.* |
|---|---|

---

**6. Scaffolding connections between the reading and children's experiences or other knowledge**

Greta and her Mom

| Mom: | (pointing) *So there is the stalk, it's like between an umbilical cord* (inaudible) *and the bean.* |
|---|---|

Jennifer and her Mom

| Mom: | (reads) "A FIELD OF BEANS." (to Jennifer) *Do we have these kind of fields in Indiana?* |
|---|---|
| **Jennifer:** | *Aha. Daddy used to live in it once, but it had beans and corn.* |

| Mom: | *Do you remember what kind of beans?* |
|---|---|
| **Jennifer:** | *Um, no! Actually . . .* (pauses as she is thinking) |
| **Mom** | (whispering in Jennifer's ear) *S . . . s . . . s. . . oy beans?* |
| **Jennifer:** | *Soy beans!* |

7. **Drawing attention to text in general (e.g., by running finger through words and sentences)**

   Xique and his Mom (observer's notes)

   While reading the book, Mom asks Xique to read words and to identify a question mark and its meaning. Mom often points to specific words and pictures.

8. **Drawing attention to sounds of letters or words**

   Marianna and her Mom

   | **Mom:** | (points to the word "sprouting" on p. 28 of the book) *Look at the top. S . . . P . . . R . . . outing!* |
   |---|---|

   Michael and his Mom

   | **Mom:** | (p. 4) *That's beans. That's a little b.* |
   |---|---|
   | **Michael:** | (p. 8) *That says steam.* |
   | **Mom:** | *Stem.* |
   | **Michael:** | *Stem.* |
   | **Mom:** | *It seems like it says steam, but there's no A in it.* |

9. **Drawing attention to new words and defining them**

   Cara and her Dad

   | **Dad:** | *What's that word? It's what birds do when they come out of their shell?* |
   |---|---|
   | **Cara:** | *Hatch.* |
   | **Dad:** | *That's what hatch is. To be born out of an egg.* |

   Christopher and his Mom

   | **Mom:** | (reads on p. 30) "RICH PEOPLE WOULD NOT EAT FAVA BEANS BECAUSE THEY THOUGHT THEY WOULD DAMAGE THEIR SIGHT." |
   |---|---|

*(Continued)*

**Table 7.2**   (Continued)

| | |
|---|---|
| **Christopher:** | *What's sight?* |
| **Mom:** | *How they see. They thought they would damage their eyes and they wouldn't be able to see.* |

**10. Responding to child and acknowledging his or her comments and questions**
Larissa and her Dad

| | |
|---|---|
| **Dad:** | (reads on p. 11) "FLOWER BUDS BEGIN TO FORM." |
| **Larissa:** | *Just like buckeyes, daddy.* |
| **Dad:** | *Just like buckeyes!* |

Jillian and her Mom

| | |
|---|---|
| **Mom:** | (reads about the stalk and asks) *See the beans and the little tiny stalks?* |
| **Jillian:** | *It kinda looks like hearts.* |
| **Mom:** | *They do look like hearts.* |

**11. Using the text to support children's mathematical knowledge**

Jennifer and her Mom (counting and estimation)

| | |
|---|---|
| **Mom:** | *How many pods do you think there are?* |
| **Jennifer:** | (counts) *1, 2, 3 . . .* |
| **Mom:** | (prompting for estimation) *Well, how many do you think you're gonna have?* |
| **Jennifer:** | *Can I count?* |
| **Mom:** | *No, we're not going to count right now.* |
| **Jennifer:** | *Um, 27!* |
| **Mom:** | *27?* |
| **Jennifer:** | *That's a lot!* |
| **Mom:** | *Aha!* |

Christopher and his Mom (making size comparisons)

| | |
|---|---|
| **Mom:** | (reads) "IN JUST FOUR MONTHS A FAVA BEAN GROWS FROM A SEED TO A PLANT AS TALL AS AN ADULT PERSON." (to Christopher) *It's a tall plant, isn't it?* |

| Christopher: | *What about, like dad?* |
|---|---|
| **Mom:** | *I don't know if they grow that tall or not. That'd be pretty tall, wouldn't it?* |
| **Christopher:** | *Yeah!* |

## IN CONCLUSION

Informational texts are resources that fulfill important functions in the course of addressing children's thirst for new knowledge. Parent-child shared reading and conversations about informational books are important ways to engage children in thinking, remembering, and learning about topics of interest to them. Interactional strategies, intended to support children's language development and background knowledge, when used both at home and school, can serve as common tools for parents and teachers to enrich and provide continuity in children's learning experiences.

## CHAPTER 7 APPLICATIONS FOR PRACTICE

### Try-It-On Activities

The following suggested activities require that you try ideas presented in this chapter in your classroom.

1. Survey your students and their families to find out about their shared reading routines, favorite books, and needs. Who reads at home? What is read? What kinds of books need to be provided? What types of parent development need to be done?

2. Using the examples provided in Chapter 7 for how to support family-child interaction around informational texts, how could you change your current school-home communications or create a new plan for school-home

communications to support children's interactions with quality informational texts at home? Refer to Chapter 4 to review quality considerations.

## FOR DISCUSSION AND REFLECTION

1. Discuss the finding that there is more talk during shared reading. Why is this finding so important? Consider different aspects of the child's development: cognitive (i.e., thinking skills), socioemotional, motivational, and social.

2. Reflect upon the possibilities of more reading of informational text at school and home. Discuss three to five positive outcomes that could be achieved by more breadth and balance in the genres young children are read. How are these possibilities supported by the research the authors provide in Chapter 7? Throughout this book?

## HIGHLY RECOMMENDED READING AND WEBSITE

Bennett-Armistead, V. S., Duke, N., & Moses, A. (2007). *Beyond bedtime stories: A parent's guide to promoting reading, writing, and other literacy skills from birth to 5.* New York, NY: Scholastic.

Reading Rockets is funded by a grant from the U.S. Department of Education, Office of Special Education Programs. The Reading Rockets website parent link is at http://www.readingrockets.org/audience/parents/

# References for Children's Books

Aliki. (1985). *My visit to the dinosaurs.* New York, NY: HarperCollins.

Benfanti, R. (2002). *Hide, Clyde.* New York, NY: ipicturebooks.

Carle, E. (1987). *The very hungry caterpillar.* New York, NY: Philomel Books.

Clyne, M., & Griffiths, R. (2005). *Fins, wings, and legs.* Parsippany, NJ: Celebration Press.

Crampton, G. (1945). *Tootle.* New York, NY: Random House.

dePaola, T. (1984). *The popcorn book.* New York, NY: Holiday House.

Douglas, L. G. (2002). *What is a lever?* New York: Children's Press.

Fowler, A. (2001). *Simple machines.* New York, NY: Children's Press.

Halpern, M. (2002). *All about light.* Washington, DC: National Geographic.

Hughes, M. (2005). *What is an ocean?* Chicago, IL: Heinemann.

James, S. (1991). *Dear Mr. Blueberry.* New York, NY: Aladdin.

Kamma, A. (2004). *If you lived when there was slavery in America.* New York, NY: Scholastic.

Piper, W. (1976). *The little engine that could.* New York, NY: Platt & Munk.

Pitino, D. M. (2006). *Playground science.* Waterbury, CT: Abrams.

Polette, N. (2004). *Isn't it strange?* Rocky River, OH: Kaeden Books.

Ramirez, M. (2007). *Force and motion.* Waterbury, CT: Abrams.

Robinson, C. (1999). *Dolphins.* Chicago, IL: Heinemann.

Royston, A. (1998). *Life cycle of a bean.* Chicago, IL: Heinemann.

Santiago, R. O. (2006). *Amazing plants.* Waterbury, CT: Abrams.

Swartz, S. L. (2002). *Fish that hide.* Parsippany, NJ: Dominie Press.

Yu, N. (2006). *Science is everywhere.* Waterbury, CT: Abrams.

Wong, G. (2001). *Plants and animals live here.* Washington, DC: National Geographic Society.

# References for Research Sources

Abbott, R. D., Berninger, V. W., & Fayol, M. (2010). Longitudinal relationships of levels of language in writing and between writing and reading in grades 1 to 7. *Journal of Educational Psychology, 102*, 281–298.

ACT. (2006). *Reading between the lines: What the ACT reveals about college readiness in reading.* Iowa City, IA: Author. Retrieved from http://www.act.org/research/policymakers/reports/reading .html

Alexander, P. A. (1997). Knowledge-seeking and self-schema: A case for the motivational dimensions of exposition. *Educational Psychologist, 32*, 83–94.

Ambruster, B., Lehr, F., & Osborn, J. (2008). *Put reading first: Kindergarten through grade 3.* Washington, DC: National Institute for Literacy. Retrieved from http://www.edpubs.gov/Product_ Detail.aspx?SearchTerm=ED004380P

Anderson, R. C., Hiebert, E. H., Scott, J. A., & Wilkinson, I. A. G. (1985). *Becoming a nation of readers: The report of the Commission on Reading.* Washington, DC: U.S. Department of Education.

Andre, T., Whigham, M., Hendrickson, A., & Chambers, S. (1999). Competency beliefs, positive affect, and gender stereotypes of elementary students and their parents about science versus other school subjects. *Journal of Research in Science Teaching, 36*, 719–747.

Ansberry, K. R., & Morgan, E. (2005). *Picture perfect science lessons: Using children's books to guide inquiry, 3–6.* Arlington, VA: NSTA Press.

Apel, K. (2009). The acquisition of mental orthographic representations for reading and spelling development. *Communication Disorders Quarterly, 31,* 42–52.

Aunola, K., Leskinen, E., Onatsu-Arvilommi, T., & Nurmi, J. (2002). Three methods for studying developmental changes: A case of reading skills and self-concept. *British Journal of Educational Psychology, 72,* 343–364.

Baker, D. R. (1998). Equity issues in science education. In B. J. Frazer & K. G. Tobin (Eds.), *International handbook of science education* (pp. 869–895). Lancaster, UK: Kluwer Academic.

Baker, L., & Saul W. (1994). Considering science and language arts connections: A study of teacher cognition. *Journal of Research in Science Teaching, 31,* 1023–1037.

Baram-Tsabari, A., Sethi, R. J., Bry, L., & Yarden, A. (2006). Using questions sent to an ask-a-scientist site to identify children's interest in science. *Science Education, 90,* 1050–1072.

Baram-Tsabari, A., & Yarden, A. (2005). Characterizing children's spontaneous interests in science and technology. *International Journal of Science Education, 27,* 803–826.

Barman, C. R. (1999). Students' views about scientists and school science: Engaging K–8 teachers in a national study. *Journal of Science Teacher Education, 10,* 43–54.

Beals, D. E., & Snow, C. E. (1994). Thunder is when the angels are upstairs bowling: Narratives and explanations at the dinner table. *Journal of Narrative and Live History, 4,* 331–351.

Beck, I. L., & McKeown, M. G. (2007). Increasing young, low-income children's oral vocabulary repertoires through rich and focused instruction. *The Elementary School Journal, 107,* 251–271.

Berkin, A. (2012). Quick guide to the common core: Key expectations explained. In *Education Week. Spotlight: On literacy and the common core* (pp. 15–16). Retrieved from http://www.edweek.org/ew/marketplace/products/spotlight-literacy-common-core-standards.html

Berninger, V. W., Vaughan, K., Abbott, R. D., Begay, K., Coleman, K. B., Curtin, G., . . . Graham, S. (2002). Teaching spelling and composition alone and together: Implications for the simple view of writing. *Journal of Educational Psychology, 92,* 291–304.

Bersh, L. C. (2013). The curricular value of teaching about immigration through picture book thematic text sets. *The Social Studies, 104,* 47–56.

Best, R. M., Floyd, R. G., & McNamara, D. S. (2008). Differential competencies contributing to children's comprehension of narrative and expository texts. *Reading Psychology, 29,* 137–164.

Blewitt, P., Rump, K. M., Shealy, S. E., & Cook, S. A. (2009). Shared book reading: When and how questions affect young children's world learning. *Journal of Educational Psychology, 101,* 294–304.

Blum-Kulka S., & Snow, C. E. (1992). Developing autonomy for tellers, tales, and telling in family narrative events. *Journal of Narrative and Life History, 20,* 187–217.

Brabham, E. G., Boyd, P., & Edgington, W. D. (2010). Sorting it out: Elementary students' responses to fact and fiction in informational storybooks as read-alouds for science and social studies. *Reading Research and Instruction, 39,* 265–290.

Brabham, E. G., & Lynch-Brown, C. (2002). Effects of teachers' reading-aloud styles on vocabulary acquisition and comprehension of students in the early elementary grades. *Journal of Educational Psychology, 94,* 465–473.

Brenna, B. (2008). Breaking stereotypes with children's fiction: Seeking protagonists with special needs. *International Journal of Special Education, 23*(1), 100–103.

Brophy, J., & Alleman, J. (2009). Meaningful social studies for elementary students. *Teachers and Teaching Theory and Practice, 15,* 357–376.

Brotman, J. S., & Moore, F. M. (2008). Girls and science: A review of four themes in the science education literature. *Journal of Research in Science Teaching, 45,* 971–1002.

Brown, A. L. (1997). Transforming schools into communities of thinking and learning about serious matters. *American Psychologist, 32,* 399–413.

Buldu, M. (2006). Young children's perceptions of scientists: A preliminary study. *Educational Research, 48,* 121–132.

Callanan, M. A., & Jipson, J. L (2001). Explanatory conversations and young children's developing scientific literacy. In K. Crowley, C. D. Schunn, & T. Okada (Eds.), *Designing for science: Implications from everyday, classroom, and professional settings* (pp. 19–49). Mahwah, NJ: Erlbaum.

Callanan, M. A., & Oakes, L. M. (1992). Preschoolers' questions and parents' explanations: Causal thinking in everyday activity. *Cognitive Development, 7,* 213–233.

Caswell, L. J., & Duke, N. K. (1998). Non-narrative as a catalyst for literacy development. *Language Arts, 75,* 108–117.

Cervetti, G. N., Bravo, M. A., Hiebert, E. H., & Pearson, P. D. (2009). Text genre and science content: Ease of reading, comprehension, and reader preference. *Reading Psychology, 30,* 487–511.

Chall, J. S., & Dale, E. (1995). *Readability revisited: The new Dale-Chall readability formula.* Brookline, MA: Brookline Books.

Chapman, J. W., Tunmer, W. E., & Pronchow, J. E. (2000). Early reading-related skills and performance, reading self-concept, and the development of academic self-concept: A longitudinal study. *Journal of Educational Psychology, 92,* 703–708.

Chin, C., Brown, D. E., & Bruce, B. C. (2002). Student-generated questions: A meaningful aspect of learning in science. *International Journal of Science Education, 24,* 521–549.

Chouinard, M. M. (2007). Children's questions: A mechanism for cognitive development. *Monographs of the Society for Research in Child Development, 72*(1, Serial No. 286).

Conrad, N. J. (2008). From reading to spelling and spelling to reading: Transfer goes both ways. *Journal of Educational Psychology, 100,* 869–878.

Corriveau, K. H., & Harris, P. (2009). Choosing your informant: Weighing familiarity and recent accuracy. *Developmental Science, 12,* 426–437.

Corriveau, K. H., Kim, A. L., Schwalen, C. E., & Harris, P. L. (2009). Abraham Lincoln and Harry Potter: Children's differentiation between historical and fantasy characters. *Cognition, 113,* 213–225.

Cutler, L., & Graham, S. (2008). Primary grade writing instruction: A national survey. *Journal of Educational Psychology, 100,* 907–919.

Davis, E. A. (1932). The form and function of children's questions. *Child Development, 3,* 57–74.

Dawson, C. (2000). Upper primary boys' and girls' interests in science: Have they changed since 1980? *International Journal of Science Education, 22,* 557–570.

De Temple, J. D., & Snow, C. E. (2003). Learning words from books. In A. van Kleeck, S. A. Stahl, & E. B. Bauer (Eds.), *On reading books to children* (pp. 16–36). Mahwah, NJ: Erlbaum.

DeMarie, D., Norman, A., & Abshier, D. W. (2000). Age and experience influence different verbal and nonverbal measures of children's scripts for the zoo. *Cognitive Development, 15,* 241–262.

Dickinson, D. K. (2001). Book reading in preschool classrooms: Is recommended practice common? In D. K. Dickinson & P. O. Tabors (Eds.), *Beginning literacy with language* (pp. 175–203). Baltimore, MA: Brooks.

Dockrell, J. E., Braisby, N., & Best, R. M. (2007). Children's acquisition of science terms: Simple exposure is insufficient. *Learning and Instruction, 17,* 577–594.

Donovan, C. A. (2001). Children's development and control of written story and informational genres: Insights from one elementary school. *Research in the Teaching of English, 35,* 394–447.

Donovan, C. A., & Smolkin, L. B. (2001). Genre and other factors influencing teachers' book selections for science instruction. *Reading Research Quarterly, 36,* 412–440.

Donovan, C. A., & Smolkin, L. B. (2002). Considering genre, content, and visual features in the selection of trade books for science instruction. *The Reading Teacher, 55,* 502–520.

Donovan, C. A., & Smolkin, L. B. (2011). Supporting informational writing in the elementary grades. *The Reading Teacher, 64,* 406–416.

Donovan, C. A., Smolkin, L. B., & Lomax, R. G. (2000). Beyond the independent-level text: Considering the reader-text match in first-graders' self-selections during recreational reading. *Reading Psychology, 21,* 309–333.

Duke, N. K. (2000). 3.6 minutes per day: The scarcity of informational texts in first grade. *Reading Research Quarterly, 35,* 202–224.

Duke, N. K., & Kays, N. (1998). "Can I say 'once upon a time'?": Kindergarten children developing knowledge of information book language. *Early Childhood Research Quarterly, 13,* 205–318.

Duplass, J. A. (2007). Elementary social studies: Trite, disjointed, and in need of reform? *The Social Studies, 4,* 137–177.

Eccles, J. (2007). Where are all the women? Gender differences in participation in physical science and engineering. In S. J. Ceci & W. M. Williams (Eds.), *Why aren't more women in science?* (pp. 199–210). Washington, DC: American Psychological Association.

Egan, K. (1988). *Primary understanding: Education in early childhood.* New York, NY: Routledge.

Evans, M A., & Saint-Aubin, J. (2005). What children are looking at during shared storybook reading: Evidence from eye movement monitoring. *Psychological Science, 16,* 913–920.

Fan, X., & Chen, M. (2001). Parental involvement and students' academic achievement: A meta-analysis. *Educational Psychology Review, 13,* 1–22.

Finson, K. D. (2002). Drawing a scientist: What we do and do not know after fifty years of drawings. *School Science and Mathematics, 102,* 335–345.

Fleener, C. E., Morrison, S., Linek, W. M., & Rasinski, T. V. (1997). Recreational reading choices: How do children select books? In W. M. Linek & E. G. Sturtevant (Eds.), *Exploring literacy* (pp. 75–84). Pittsburg, KS: College Reading Association.

Fletcher, K. L., & Reese, E. (2005). Picture book reading with young children: A conceptual framework. *Developmental Review, 25,* 64–103.

Ford, D. J. (2004). Scaffolding preservice teachers' evaluation of children's science literature: Attention to science-focused genres and use. *Journal of Science Teacher Education, 12,* 133–153.

Ford, D. J. (2006). Representations of science within children's trade books. *Journal of Research in Science Teaching, 43,* 214–235.

Ford, D. J., Brickhouse, N. W., Lottero-Perdue, P., & Kittleson, J. (2006). Elementary girls' science reading at home and school. *Science Education, 90,* 270–288.

Gallimore, R., & Goldenberg, C. (2001). Analyzing cultural models and settings to connect minority achievement and school improvement research. *Educational Psychologist, 36,* 45–56.

Gallimore, R., & Tharp, R. (2001). Teaching mind in society: Teaching, schooling, and literate discourse. In L. C. Moll (Ed.), *Vygotsky and education: Instructional implications and applications of sociohistorical psychology* (pp. 175–205). Cambridge, UK: Cambridge University Press.

Ganea, P. A., Ma, L., & DeLoache, J. S. (2011). Young children's learning and transfer of biological information from picture books to real animals. *Child Development, 82,* 1421–1433.

Ganea, P. A., Pickard, M. B., & DeLoache, J. S. (2008). Transfer between picture books and the real world by very young children. *Journal of Cognition and Development, 9,* 46–66.

Gee, J. P. (2004). Language in the science classroom: Academic social languages as the heart of school-based literacy. In E. W. Saul (Ed.), *Crossing borders in literacy and language instruction: Perspectives on theory and practice* (pp. 13–32). Arlington, VA: NSTA Press.

Gelman, S. A. (2009). Learning from others: Children's construction of concepts. *Annual Review of Psychology, 60,* 115–140.

Gentry, J. R. (2005). Instructional techniques for emerging writers and special needs students at kindergarten and grade 1 levels. *Reading and Writing Quarterly, 21,* 113–134.

Gerde, H. K., Bingham, G. E., & Wasik, B. A. (2012). Writing in early childhood classrooms: Guidance for best practices. *Early Childhood Education Journal, 40,* 351–359.

Gewertz, C. (2012). Rid of memorization, history lessons build analytical skills. In *Education Week. Spotlight: On literacy and the common core* (pp. 9–11). Retrieved from http://www.edweek.org/ew/marketplace/products/spotlight-literacy-common-core-standards.html

Goldman, S. R., & Bisanz, G. L. (2002). Toward a functional analysis of scientific genres: Implications for understanding and learning processes. In J. Otero, J. A. Leon, & A. C. Grasser (Eds.), *The psychology of science text comprehension* (pp. 19–50). Mahwah, NJ: Erlbaum.

Graesser, A., Golding, J. M., & Long, D. L. (1991). Narrative representation and comprehension. In R. Barr, M. L. Kamil, P. Mosenthal, & P. D. Pearson (Eds.). *Handbook of reading research* (Vol. II, pp. 171–205). Mahwah, NJ: Erlbaum.

Graham, S., Berninger, V., & Abbott, R. (2012). Are attitudes toward writing and reading separable constructs? A study with primary grade children. *Reading and Writing Quarterly, 28,* 51–69.

Graham, S., Berninger, V., & Fan, W. (2007). The structural relationship between writing attitude and writing achievements in first and third grade students. *Contemporary Educational Psychology, 32,* 516–536.

Graham, S., & Harris, K. R. (2000). The role of self-regulation and transcription skills in writing and writing development. *Educational Psychologist, 35,* 3–12.

Graham, S., Harris, K. R., & Fink, B. (2000). Is handwriting causally related to learning to write? Treatment of handwriting problems in beginning writers. *Journal of Educational Psychology, 92,* 620–633.

Greenfield, T. A. (1997). Gender- and grade-level differences in science interest and participation. *Science Education, 81,* 259–276.

Guthrie, J. T., Hoa, A. L. W., Wigfield, A., Tonks, S. M., Humenick, N. M., & Littles, E. (2007). Reading motivation and reading comprehension growth in the later elementary years. *Contemporary Educational Psychology, 32,* 282–313.

Hall, K. M., Sabey, B. L., & McLellan, M. (2005). Expository text comprehension: Helping primary-grade teachers use expository texts to full advantage. *Reading Psychology, 26,* 211–234.

Harkrader, M. A., & Moore, R. (1997). Literature preferences of fourth-graders. *Reading Research and Instruction, 36,* 325–339.

Hebert, M., Gillespie, A., & Graham, S. (2013). Comparing effects of different writing activities on reading comprehension: A meta-analysis. *Reading and Writing, 26,* 111–138.

Helmke, A., & van Aken, M. A. G. (1995). The causal ordering of academic achievement and self-concept of ability during elemenary school: A longitudinal study. *Journal of Educational Psychology, 87,* 624–637.

Hiebert, E. H., & Cervetti, G. N. (2011). *What differences in narrative and informational texts mean for the learning and instruction of vocabulary* (Research Report No. 11.01). Retrieved from http:// www.textproject.org/research/reading-research-reports/what-differences-in-narrative-and-informational-texts-mean-for-the-learning-and-instruction-of-vocabulary

Hirsch, E. D., Jr. (2006). *The knowledge deficit: Closing the shocking education gap for American children.* New York, NY: Houghton Mifflin.

Inagaki, K., & Hatano, G. (2006). Young children's conception of the biological world. *Current Directions in Psychological Science, 15,* 177–181.

Institute for a Competitive Workforce. (2011). *Life in the 21st century workforce: A national perspective.* Washington, DC: U.S. Chamber of Commerce. Retrieved from http://icw.uschamber.com/ publication/life-21st-century-workforce-national-perspective

Institute for a Competitive Workforce. (2012). *Help wanted 2012: Addressing the skills gap.* Washington, DC: U.S. Chamber of Commerce. Retrieved from http://icw.uschamber.com/ publication/help-wanted-2012-addressing-skills-gap

International Reading Association. (2012). *Literacy implementation guidance for the ELA Common Core State Standards.* Washington, DC: Author. Retrieved from http://www.reading.org/Libraries/ association-documents/ira_ccss_guidelines.pdf

Jetton, T. L. (1994). Information-driven versus story driven: What children remember when they are read informational stories. *Reading Psychology, 12,* 109–130.

Jones, A. T., & Kirk, C. M. (1990). Gender differences in students' interests in applications of school physics. *Physics Education, 25,* 308–313.

Jones, M. G., Howe, A., & Rua, M. J. (2000). Gender differences in students' experiences, interests, and attitudes toward science and scientists. *Science Education, 84,* 180–192.

Justice, L. M., Kaderavek, J. N., Fan, X., Sofka, A., & Hunt A. (2009). Accelerating preschoolers' early literacy development through classroom-based teacher-child storybook reading and explicit print referencing. *Language, Speech, and Hearing Services in Schools, 40,* 67–85.

Justice, L. M., Pullen, P. C., & Pence, K. (2008). Influence of verbal and nonverbal references to print on preschoolers' visual attention to print during storybook reading. *Developmental Psychology, 44*, 855–866.

Kamberelis, G. (1999). Genre development and learning: Children writing stories, science reports, and poems. *Research in the Teaching of English, 33*, 403–460.

Kamil, M. L., & Bernhard, E. B. (2004). The science of reading and the reading of science: Successes, failures and promises in the search for prerequisite reading skills for science. In E. W. Saul (Ed.), *Crossing borders in literacy and language instruction: Perspectives on theory and practice* (pp. 123–139). Arlington, VA: NSTA Press.

Karweit, N. (1989). The effects of a story-reading program on the vocabulary and story comprehension skills of disadvantaged prekindergarten and kindergarten students. *Early Education and Development, 1*, 105–114.

Karweit, N., & Wasik, B. A. (1996). The effects of story reading programs on literacy and language development of disadvantaged preschoolers. *Journal of Education for Students Placed At Risk, 1*, 319–348.

Kraemer, L., McCabe, P., & Sinatra, R. (2012). The effects of read-alouds of expository text on first graders' listening comprehension and book choice. *Literacy Research and Instruction, 51*, 165–178.

Kuhn, D. (2004). What is scientific thinking and how does it develop? In U. Goswami (Ed.), *Blackwell handbook of childhood cognitive development* (pp. 371–393). Malden, MA: Blackwell.

Leal, D. J. (1994). A comparison of third-grade children's listening comprehension of scientific information using an information book and an informational storybook. In C. K. Kinzer & D. J. Leu (Eds.), *Multidimensional aspects of literacy research, theory, and practice: Forty-third yearbook of the National Reading Conference* (pp. 137–145). Chicago IL: National Reading Conference.

Lee, O. (2002). Promoting scientific inquiry with elementary students from diverse cultures and languages. In W. G. Secada (Ed.), *Review of research in education: Vol. 26.* Washington, DC: American Educational Research Association.

Lee, O., Fradd, S. H., & Sutman, F. X. (1995). Science knowledge and cognitive strategy use among culturally and linguistically diverse students. *Journal of Research in Science Teaching, 32*, 797–816.

Lee, P. C. (2012). The human child's nature orientation. *Child Development Perspectives, 6*, 193–198.

Lee, Y., Lee, J., Han, M., & Schickedanz, J. A. (2011). Comparison of preschoolers' narratives, the classroom book environment, and teacher attitudes toward literacy practices in Korea and the United States. *Early Education and Development, 22*, 234–255.

Leung, C. B. (2008). Preschoolers' acquisition of scientific vocabulary through repeated read-aloud events, retellings, and hands-on science activities. *Reading Psychology, 29,* 165–193.

Mantzicopoulos, P., & Patrick, H. (2010). "The seesaw is a machine that goes up and down": Young children's narrative responses to science-related informational text. *Early Education and Development, 21,* 412–444.

Mantzicopoulos, P., & Patrick, H. (2011). Reading picture books and learning science: Engaging young children with informational text. *Theory into Practice, 50,* 269–276.

Mantzicopoulos, P., & Patrick, H. (2012). *The Scientific Literacy Project.* Unpublished data.

Mantzicopoulos, P., Patrick, H., & Smarapungavan, A. (2013). Science literacy in school and home contexts: Kindergarteners' science achievement and motivation. *Cognition and Instruction, 31,* 62–119.

Mantzicopoulos, P., Samarapungavan, A., & Patrick, H. (2009). "We learn how to predict and be a scientist": Early science experiences and kindergarten children's social meanings about science. *Cognition and Instruction, 27,* 312–369.

Maria, K., & Junge, K. (1994). A comparison of fifth graders' comprehension and retention of scientific information using a science textbook and an informational storybook. In C. K. Kinzer & D. J. Leu (Eds.), *Multidimensional aspects of literacy research, theory, and practice. Forty-third yearbook of the National Reading Conference* (pp. 146–152). Chicago IL: National Reading Conference.

Marinak, B. A., & Gambrell, L. B. (2009). Ways to teach about information text. *Social Studies and the Young Learner, 22*(1), 19–22.

Martinez, M. G., & Teale, W. H. (1993). Teacher storybook reading style: A comparison of six teachers. *Research in the Teaching of English, 27,* 175–199.

Marx, R. W., & Harris, C. J. (2006). No Child Left Behind and science education: Opportunities, challenges, and risks. *Elementary School Journal, 106,* 467–477.

Mayer, D. A. (1995). How can we best use literature in teaching? *Science and Children, 32*(6), 15–19, 43.

McClure, A. A., & Zitlow, C. S. (1991). Not just the facts: Aesthetic response in elementary content area studies. *Language Arts, 68,* 27–33.

McCutchen, D. (2006). Cognitive factors in the development of children's writing. In C. A. MacArthur, S. Graham, & J. Fitzgerald (Eds.), *Handbook of writing research* (pp. 115–130). New York, NY: Guilford.

McGill-Franzen, A. (Ed.). (2010). The National Early Literacy Panel report: Summary, commentary and reflections on policies and practices to improve children's early literacy [Special issue]. *Educational Researcher, 39*(4).

Merisuo-Storm, T. (2006). Girls and boys like to read and write different texts. *Scandinavian Journal of Educational Research, 50,* 111–125.

Meyer, D. K. (1993). What is scaffolded instruction? Definitions, distinguishing features, and misnomers. C. J. Kinzer & D. J. Leu (Eds.), *Forty-second yearbook of the National Reading Conference* (pp. 41–53). Chicago, IL: National Reading Conference.

Meyer, D. K., & Turner, J. C. (2002). Using instructional discourse analysis to study the scaffolding of student self-regulation. *Educational Psychologist, 37,* 17–25.

Miller, P. H., Blessing, J. S., & Schwartz, S. (2006). Gender differences in high-school students' views about science. *International Journal of Science Education, 28,* 363–381.

Mohr, K. A. (2003). Children's choices: A comparison of book preferences between Hispanic and non-Hispanic first-graders. *Reading Psychology, 24,* 163–176.

Mohr, K. A. (2006). Children's choices for recreational reading: A three-part investigation of selection preferences, rationales, and processes. *Journal of Literacy Research, 38,* 81–104.

Moje, E. B. (2008). Foregrounding the disciplines in secondary literacy teaching and learning: A call for change. *Journal of Adolescent and Adult Literacy, 52,* 96–107.

Mol, S. E., Bus, A. G., & de Jong, M. T. (2009). Interactive book reading in early education: A tool to stimulate print knowledge as well as oral language. *Review of Educational Research, 79,* 979–1007.

Monte-Sano, C. (2010). Disciplinary literacy in history: An exploration of the historical nature of adolescents' writing. *Journal of the Learning Sciences, 19,* 539–568.

Monte-Sano, C. (2011). Beyond reading comprehension and summary: Learning to read and write in history by focusing on evidence, perspective, and interpretation. *Curriculum Inquiry, 41,* 212–249.

Morrow, L. M. (1990). Assessing children's understanding of story through their construction and reconstruction of narrative. In L. M. Morrow & J. F. Smith (Eds.), *Assessment for instruction in early literacy* (pp. 110–134). Englewood Cliffs, NJ: Prentice Hall.

Morrow, L. M., & Brittain, R. (2003). The nature of storybook reading in the elementary school: Current practices. In A. van Kleek, S. A. Stahl, & E. B. Bauer (Eds.), *On reading books to children* (pp. 140–158). Mahwah, NJ: Erlbaum.

Morrow, L. M., O'Connor, E. M., & Smith, J. K. (1990). Effects of a story reading program on the literacy development of at-risk kindergarten children. *Journal of Reading Behavior, 22,* 255–275.

Moss, B. (1997). A qualitative assessment of first graders' retelling of expository text. *Reading Research and Instruction, 37,* 1–13.

Moss, B. (2008). The information text gap: The mismatch between non-narrative text types in basal readers and 2009 NAEP recommended guidelines. *Journal of Literacy Research, 20,* 201–219.

Mullis, I. V. S., Martin, M. O., Kennedy, A. M., & Foy, P. (2007). *PIRLS 2006 international report: IEA's progress in international reading literacy study in primary schools in 40 countries.* Boston, MA: TIMSS & PIRLS International Study Center.

Murachver, T., Pipe, M. E., Gordon, R., Owens, L., & Fivush, R. (1996). Do, show, and tell: Children's event memories acquired through direct experience, observation, and stories. *Child Development, 67,* 3029–3044.

National Academy of Sciences, National Academy of Engineering, & Institute of Medicine. (2010). *Rising above the gathering storm, revisited: Rapidly approaching category 5.* Washington, DC: National Academies Press. Retrieved from http://www.nap.edu/catalog .php?record_id=12999

National Association for the Education of Young Children & International Reading Association. (1998). *Learning to read and write: Developmentally appropriate practices for young children* (Joint Position Paper). Washington, DC: Authors.

National Association for the Education of Young Children & National Association of Early Childhood Specialists in State Departments of Education. (2003). *Early childhood curriculum, assessment, and program evaluation* (Joint Position Paper). Washington, DC: Authors.

National Center for Educational Statistics. (2012). *The nation's report card. Writing 2011: National Assessment of Educational Progress at grades 8 and 12.* Washington, DC: U.S. Department of Education. Retrieved from http://nces.ed.gov/pubsearch/pubsinfo .asp?pubid=2012470

National Council for the Social Studies. (2012a). *Notable social studies trade books for young people.* Silver Spring, MD: Author. Retrieved from http://www.ncss.org/system/files/notable2011.pdf

National Council for the Social Studies. (2012b). *Powerful and purposeful teaching and learning in elementary school social studies.* Silver Spring, MD: Author. Retrieved from http://www.ncss.org/positions/powerfulandpurposeful

National Council of Teachers of English. (2004). *NCTE beliefs about the teaching of writing.* Urbana, IL: Author. Retrieved from http://www.ncte.org/positions/statements/writingbeliefs

National Council of Teachers of English & International Reading Association. (1996). *Standards for the English language arts.* Urbana, IL: NCTE and Newark, DE: International Reading Association. Retrieved from: http://www.ncte.org/standards

National Early Literacy Panel. (2008). *Developing early literacy: Report of the National Early Literacy Panel.* Washington, DC: National Institute for Literacy. Retrieved from http://lincs.ed.gov/publications/pdf/NELPReport09.pdf

National Governors Association Center for Best Practices & Council of Chief State School Officers. (2010). *Common core state standards.* Washington, DC: Authors.

National Research Council. (2007). *Taking science to school: Learning and teaching science in grades K–8.* Washington, DC: National Academies Press. Retrieved from http://www.nap.edu/catalog.php?record_id=11625

National Research Council. (2010). *Exploring the intersection of science education and 21st century skills.* Washington, DC: National Academies Press. Retrieved from http://www.nap.edu/catalog.php?record_id=12771

National Research Council. (2012). *A framework for K–12 science education: Practices, crosscutting concepts, and core ideas.* Washington, DC: National Academies Press. Retrieved from http://www.nap.edu/catalog.php?record_id=13165

National Science Teachers Association. (2011). *Outstanding science trade books for students K–12: 2011.* Arlington, VA: Author. Retrieved from http://www.nsta.org/publications/ostb/ostb2011.aspx

Nelson, K., & Fivush, R. (2004). The emergence of autobiographical memory: A social cultural developmental theory. *Psychological Review, 111,* 486–511.

Ness, M. (2011). Teachers' use of and attitudes toward informational text in K–5 classrooms. *Reading Psychology, 32,* 28–53.

Neuman, S. B., & Roskos, K. (2012). Helping children become more knowledgeable through text. *The Reading Teacher, 66,* 207–210.

Neutze, D. L. (2008). *Picturing science: The who, what, and where of images in children's award-winning science books.* Unpublished doctoral dissertation, University of Maryland, Baltimore.

Newkirk, T. (2000). Misreading masculinity: Speculations on the great gender gap in writing. *Language Arts, 77,* 294–300.

Norman, R. R. (2010). Picture this: Processes prompted by graphics in informational text. *Literacy Teaching and Learning, 14,* 1–39.

Norris, S. P., & Phillips, L. M. (2003). How literacy in its fundamental sense is central to scientific literacy. *Science Education, 87,* 224–240.

Norris, S. P., Phillips, L. M., Smith, M. L., Guilbert, S. M., Stange, D. M., Baker, J. J., & Weber, A. C. (2008). Learning to read scientific text: Do elementary school commercial reading programs help? *Science Education, 92,* 765–798.

Ouellette, G., & Sénéchal, M. (2008). Pathways to literacy: A study of invented spelling and its role in learning to read. *Child Development, 79,* 899–913.

Ouellette, G., Sénéchal, M., & Haley, A. (2013). Guiding children's invented spellings: A gateway into literacy learning. *Journal of Experimental Education, 81,* 261–279.

Paas, F., Renkl, A., & Sweller, J. (2003). Cognitive load theory and instructional design: Recent developments. *Educational Psychologist, 38,* 1–4.

Palincsar, A. S., & Duke, N. K. (2004). The role of text and text-reader interactions in young children's reading development and achievement. *Elementary School Journal, 105,* 183–197.

Pappas, C. C. (1991). Fostering full access to literacy by including information books. *Language Arts, 68,* 449–461.

Pappas, C. C. (1993). Is narrative "primary"? Some insights from kindergarteners' pretend readings of stories and information books. *Journal of Reading Behavior, 25,* 97–129.

Pappas, C. C. (2006). The information book genre: Its role in integrated science literacy research and practice. *Reading Research Quarterly, 41,* 226–250.

Paris, A. H., & Paris, S. G. (2003). Assessing narrative comprehension in young children. *Reading Research Quarterly, 38,* 36–76.

Patrick, H., Johnson, K. R., Mantzicopoulos, P., & Gray, D. L. (2011). "I tell them I know how to do my ABCs!": Kindergarteners' school-related conversations with parents and associations with adjustment and achievement. *Elementary School Journal, 112,* 383–405.

Patrick, H., Mantzicopoulos, P., & Smarapungavan, A. (2009a). Motivation for learning science in kindergarten: Is there a gender gap and does integrated inquiry and literacy instruction make a difference. *Journal of Research in Science Teaching, 46,* 166–191.

Patrick, H., Mantzicopoulos, P., & Samarapungavan, A. (2009b). Reading, writing, and conducting inquiry about science in kindergarten. *Young Children, 64*(6), 32–38.

Pellegrini, A. D., & Galda, L. (2003). Joint reading as a context: Explicating the ways context is created by participants. In A. van Kleeck, S. A. Stahl, & E. B. Bauer (Eds.), *On reading books to children* (pp. 321–335). Mahwah, NJ: Erlbaum.

Pellegrini, A. D., Galda, L., Jones, I., & Perlmutter, J. (1995). Joint reading between mothers and their Head Start children: Vocabulary development in two text formats. *Discourse Processes, 19,* 441–463.

Pellegrini, A. D., Perlmutter, J. C., Galda, L., & Brody, G. H. (1990). Joint reading between Black Head Start children and their mothers. *Child Development, 61,* 443–453.

Pentimonti, J. M., & Justice, L. M. (2010). Teachers' use of scaffolding strategies during read alouds in the preschool classroom. *Early Childhood Education Journal, 37,* 241–248.

Pentimonti, J. M., Zucker, T. A., Justice, L. M. (2011). What are preschool teachers reading in their classrooms? *Reading Psychology, 32,* 197–236.

Perez-Granados, D. R., & Callanan, M. A. (1997). Parents and siblings as early resources for young children's learning in Mexican-descent families. *Hispanic Journal of Behavioral Sciences, 19,* 3–33.

Piaget, J. (1955). *The language and thought of the child.* Cleveland, OH: World.

Piasta, S. B., Justice, L. M., McGinty, A. S., & Kaderavek, J. N. (2012). Increasing young children's contact with print during shared reading: Longitudinal effects on literacy achievement. *Child Development, 83,* 810–820.

Price, L. H., Bradley, B. A., & Smith, J. M. (2012). A comparison of preschool teachers' talk during storybook and information book read-alouds. *Early Childhood Research Quarterly, 27,* 426–440.

Price, L. H., van Kleek A., & Huberty, C. J. (2009). Talk during book sharing between parents and preschool children: A comparison between storybook and expository book conditions. *Reading Research Quarterly, 44,* 171–194.

Przetacznik-Gierowska, M., & Ligeza, M (1990). Cognitive and interpersonal functions of children's questions. In G. Conti-Ramsden & C. E. Snow (Eds.), *Children's language* (Vol. 7, pp. 69–101). Hillsdale, NJ: Erlbaum.

Puranik, C. S., & AlOtaiba, S. (2012). Examining the contribution of handwriting and spelling to written expression in kindergarten children. *Reading and Writing, 25,* 1523–1546.

Purcell-Gates, V., Duke, N. K., & Martineau, J. A. (2007). Learning to read and write genre-specific text: Roles for authentic experience and explicit teaching. *Reading Research Quarterly, 42,* 8–45.

Reisman, A., & Wineburg, S. (2008, September-October). Teaching the skill of contextualizing in history. *The Social Studies,* pp. 202–207.

Renninger, K. A. (2000). Individual interest and development: Implications for understanding intrinsic motivation. In C. Sansone & J. M. Harackiewicz (Eds.), *Intrinsic and extrinsic motivation: The search for optimal motivation and performance* (pp. 373–404). San Diego, CA: Academic Press.

Rice, D. C. (2002). Using trade books in teaching elementary science: Facts and fallacies. *The Reading Teacher, 55,* 552–565.

Richert, R. A., & Smith, E. I. (2011). Preschoolers' quarantining of fantasy stories. *Child Development, 82,* 1106–1119.

Richgels, D. J. (2002). Informational texts in kindergarten. *The Reading Teacher, 55,* 586–594.

Roser, N. I., & Keehn, S. (2002). Fostering thought, talk, and inquiry: Linking literature and social studies. *The Reading Teacher, 55,* 416–426.

Samarapungavan, A., Mantzicopoulos, P., & Patrick, H. (2008). Learning science through inquiry in kindergarten. *Science Education, 92,* 868–908.

Samarapungavan, A., Patrick, H., & Mantzicopoulos, P. (2011). What kindergarten students learn in inquiry-based science classrooms. *Cognition and Instruction, 29,* 416–470.

Saul, E. W. (Ed.). (2004). *Crossing borders in literacy and science instruction: Perspectives on theory and practice.* Arlington, VA: National Science Teachers Association.

Schickedanz, J. A., & McGee, L. M. (2010). The NELP report on shared story reading interventions (Chapter 4): Extending the story. *Educational Researcher, 39,* 323–329.

Schroeder, M., McKeough, A., Graham, S., Stock, H., & Bisanz, G. (2009). The contribution of trade books to early science literacy: In and out of school. *Research in Science Education, 39,* 231–250.

Schussler, E. E. (2008). From flowers to fruits: How children's books represent plant reproduction. *International Journal of Science Education, 30,* 1677–1696.

*Scientific Literacy Project.* (2009). Retrieved from http://www .purduescientificliteracyproject.org

Sénéchal, M., Ouellette, G., Pagan, S., & Lever, R. (2012). The role of invented spelling on learning to read in low-phoneme aware-ness kindergartners: A randomized-control-trial study. *Reading and Writing, 25,* 917–934.

Shanahan, T. (2006). Relations among oral language, reading, and writing development. In C. A. MacArthur, S. Graham, & J. Fitzgerald (Eds.), *Handbook of writing research* (pp. 171–183). New York, NY: Guilford.

Shanahan, T., Callison, K., Carriere, C., Duke, N. K., Pearson, P. D., Schatschneider, C., & Torgesen, J. (2010). *Improving reading com-prehension in kindergarten through 3rd grade: A practice guide* (NCEE 2010–4038). Washington, DC: National Center for Education Evaluation and Regional Assistance, Institute of Education Sciences, U.S. Department of Education. Retrieved from http://ies.ed.gov/ncee/wwc/PracticeGuide.aspx?sid=14

Shanahan, T., & Shanahan, C. (2008). Teaching disciplinary literacy to adolescents: Rethinking content-area literacy. *Harvard Educa-tional Review, 78,* 40–59.

Shymansky, J. A., Yore, L. D., & Good, R. (1991). Elementary school teachers' beliefs about and perceptions of elementary school science, science reading, science textbooks, and supportive instructional factors. *Journal of Research in Science Teaching, 28,* 437–454.

Sigel, I. E. (1986). Early experience and the development of represen-tational competence. *New Directions for Child Development, 22,* 49–65.

Sigel, I. E. (1992). The belief-behavior connection: A resolvable dilemma? In I. E. Sigel, A. McGillicuddy-DeLisi, & J. J. Goodnow (Eds.), *Parental belief systems: The psychological consequences for children* (2nd ed., pp. 433–456). Hillsdale, NJ: Erlbaum.

Sigel, I. E. (2002). The psychological distancing model: A study of the socialization of cognition. *Culture & Psychology, 8,* 189–214.

Snow, C. E., Burns, M. S., & Griffin, P. (Eds.). (1998). *Preventing reading difficulties in young children.* Washington, DC: National Academy Press.

Spache, G. D. (1978). *Good reading for poor readers.* Champaign, IL: Garrard.

Sparks, S. D. (2012). New research thinking girds core. In *Education Week. Spotlight: On literacy and the common core* (pp. 6–9). Retrieved from http://www.edweek.org/ew/marketplace/products/spotlight-literacy-common-core-standards.html

Spelke, E. S. (2005). Sex differences in intrinsic aptitude for mathematics and science? A critical review. *American Psychologist, 60,* 950–958.

Tare, M., Chiong, C., Ganea, P., & DeLoache, J. (2010). Less is more: How manipulative features affect children's learning from picture books. *Journal of Applied Developmental Psychology, 31,* 395–400.

Teale, W. H. (2003). Reading aloud to young children as a classroom instructional activity: Insights from research and practice. In A. van Kleeck, S. A. Stahl, & E. B. Bauer (Eds.), *On reading books to children* (pp. 114–139). Mahwah, NJ: Erlbaum.

Tessler, M., & Nelson, K. (1994). Making memories: The influence of joint encoding on later recall by young children. *Consciousness and Cognition, 3,* 307–326.

Tower, C. (2003). Genre development and elementary students' informational writing: A review of the literature. *Reading Research and Instruction, 42,* 14–39.

Troia, G. A., Harbaugh, A. G., Shankland, R. K., Wolbers, K. A., & Lawrence, A. M. (2013). Relationships between writing motivation, writing activity, and writing performance: Effects of grade, sex, and ability. *Reading and Writing, 26,* 17–44.

U.S. Congress Joint Economic Committee. (2012). *STEM education: Preparing for the jobs of the future.* Retrieved from http://www.jec.senate.gov/public/index.cfm?a=Files.Serve&File_id=6aaa7e1f-9586-47be-82e7-326f47658320

van Kleeck, A. (2003). Research on book sharing: Another critical look. In A. van Kleeck, S. A. Stahl, & E. B. Bauer (Eds.), *On reading books to children* (pp. 271–320). Mahwah, NJ: Erlbaum.

Vander Hart, N., Fitzpatrick, P., & Cortesa, C. (2010). In-depth analysis of handwriting curriculum and instruction in four kindergarten classrooms. *Reading and Writing, 25,* 673–699.

Vernon, S. A., & Ferreiro, E. (1999). Writing development: A neglected variable in the consideration of phonological awareness. *Harvard Educational Review, 69,* 395–415.

Vygotsky, L. S. (1978). *Mind and society: The development of higher mental processes.* Cambridge, MA: Harvard University Press.

Wasik, B. A., & Bond, M. A. (2001). Beyond the pages of a book: Interactive book reading and language development in preschool classrooms. *Journal of Educational Psychology, 93,* 243–250.

Wasta, S. (2010). Be my neighbor: Exploring sense of place through children's literature. *The Social Studies, 101,* 189–193.

Weaver III, C. A., & Kintch, W. (1991). Expository text. In R. Barr, M. L. Kamil, P. Mosenthal, & P. D. Pearson (Eds.), *Handbook of reading research* (Vol. II, pp. 230–245). Mahwah, NJ: Erlbaum.

Wells, G. (1985). Pre-school literacy-related activities and success in school. In D. Olson, N. Torrance, & A. Holdyard (Eds.), *Literacy, language, and learning* (pp. 229–255). Cambridge, UK: Cambridge University Press.

Whitehurst, G. J., Zevenbergen, A. A., Crone, D. A., Schultz, M. D., Velting, O. N., & Fischel, J. E. (1999). Outcomes of an emergent literacy intervention from Head Start through second grade. *Journal of Educational Psychology, 81,* 261–272.

Wigfield, A., & Eccles, J. S. (2002). The development of competence beliefs, expectancies for success, and achievement values from childhood through adolescence. In A. Wigfield & J. S. Eccles, (Eds.), *Development of achievement motivation* (pp. 91–120). London, UK: Academic Press.

Williams, J. P., Hall, K. M., deCani, J. S., Lauer, K. D., Stafford, K. B., & DeSisto, L. A. (2005). Expository test comprehension in the primary grade classroom. *Journal of Educational Psychology, 97,* 538–550.

Wolfe, M. B. W., & Woodwyk, J. M. (2010). Processing and memory of information presented in narrative or expository texts. *British Journal of Educational Psychology, 80,* 341–362.

Wollman-Bonilla, J. E. (2000). Teaching science writing to first graders: Genre learning and recontextualization. *Research in the Teaching of English, 35,* 35–65.

Woolley, J. D., & Cox, V. (2007). Development of beliefs about storybook reality. *Developmental Science, 10,* 681–693.

Woolley, J. D., & Van Reet, J. (2006). Effects of context on judgments concerning the reality status of novel entities. *Child Development, 77,* 1778–1793.

Worthy, J., Moorman, M., & Turner, M. (1999). What Johnny likes to read is hard to find in school. *Reading Research Quarterly, 34,* 12–25.

Yopp, R. H., & Yopp, H. K. (2000). Sharing informational text with young children. *The Reading Teacher, 53,* 410–423.

Yopp, R. H., & Yopp, H. K. (2006). Informational texts as read-alouds at school and home. *Journal of Literacy Research, 38,* 1–37.

Yopp, R. H., & Yopp, H. K. (2012). Young children's limited and narrow exposure to informational text. *The Reading Teacher, 65,* 480–490.

Yore, L. D., Bisanz, G. L., & Hand, B. M. (2003). Examining the literacy component of science literacy: 25 years of language arts and science research. *International Journal of Science Education, 25,* 689–725.

Young, J. P., & Brozo, W. G. (2001). Boys will be boys, or will they? Literacy and masculinities. *Reading Research Quarterly, 36,* 316–325.

Youngs, S., & Serafini, F. (2012). Comprehension strategies for reading historical fiction picturebooks. *The Reading Teacher, 65,* 116–124.

# Index

## CORWIN
### A SAGE Company

The Corwin logo—a raven striding across an open book—represents the union of courage and learning. Corwin is committed to improving education for all learners by publishing books and other professional development resources for those serving the field of PreK–12 education. By providing practical, hands-on materials, Corwin continues to carry out the promise of its motto: **"Helping Educators Do Their Work Better."**

# DATE DUE